Alive

ALSO BY GABRIEL WESTON

Direct Red: A Surgeon's Story
Dirty Work

Alive

An Alternative Anatomy

GABRIEL WESTON

JONATHAN CAPE
LONDON

1 3 5 7 9 10 8 6 4 2

Jonathan Cape, an imprint of Vintage, is part of the
Penguin Random House group of companies

Vintage, Penguin Random House UK, One Embassy
Gardens, 8 Viaduct Gardens, London SW11 7BW

penguin.co.uk/vintage
global.penguinrandomhouse.com

Penguin
Random House
UK

First published in Great Britain by Jonathan Cape in 2025

Typeset in 12.5/18.2pt Calluna by Jouve (UK), Milton Keynes
Printed and bound in Great Britain by Clays Ltd, Elcograf S.p.A.

The authorised representative in the EEA is Penguin Random House
Ireland, Morrison Chambers, 32 Nassau Street, Dublin D02 YH68

A CIP catalogue record for this book is available from the British Library

HB ISBN 9781787330603
TPB ISBN 9781787330610

For Sam, Hetty, Miranda and Emily

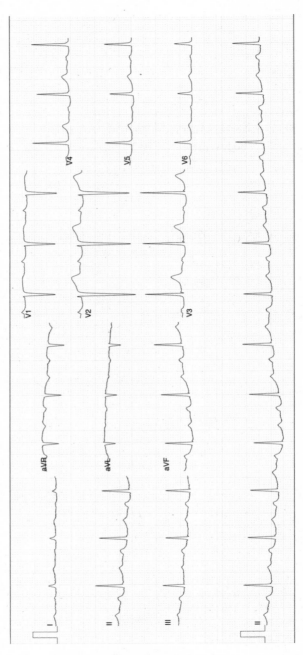

ECG Gabriel Weston 18/6/2024

Nothing makes sense until it makes sense in the body, till the body is present at the making-sense.

Jason Allen-Paisant

Contents

Dead

I arrive at the hospital just as it's getting light. The sky is purple and there's a warm, wet wind. Parking my bike where I used to as a medical student, I find the mortuary from memory, buzz and am let in by the pathology technician, who has tattoos up one arm. It's cold in reception but I am excited about seeing the dead body, the place where all anatomical explorations begin. I sign the visitors' book and go to the changing room, where I strip down to my thermals and put on a simulacrum of my surgical attire, blue scrub top and bottom, gown and cap. Then I add unfamiliar bits, plastic gauntlets from wrist to elbow, a green plastic apron which rustles to the floor, visor and two sets of gloves. There is a low wall and I step over it into white rubber boots like the ones orthopaedic surgeons wear.

A few feet away is a doorway and a barrier of black ribbons. Through this, I see stripes of room and hear the radio. I know exactly what's on the other side, but

I

when I walk in the sight of it hits me like a slap. The dead woman lies naked on a trolley in the middle of the room. Her precise stillness feels ungraspable, her life-lessness absolute. It's as if the scene has had a person-shaped silhouette cut out of it.

The pathologist gives me a nod as he approaches the table, before measuring the body's length from head to heel. This is different from the coffin length, he says, which is from head to toe. On a clipboard, he notes down distinguishing features like cannula sites and scars. Next, the technician from reception brings out a tray on legs, that reminds me of the one my grandma used for breakfast in bed, and which slots across the body in much the same way. But, instead of bacon and eggs and a flower in a glass, she tops it with a sturdy chopping board, a washing-up bowl lined with a plastic bag, and a collection of instruments. These too look familiar, like things you would find in your kitchen or garden shed and would call bread knife, ladle, hammer, chisel, scissors, skewer and ruler. There is also a scalpel called a PM40, which is like the kind I use when I'm operating, only much bigger.

Picking up the knife, the pathologist holds it per-pendicular to the skin at the base of the neck, grasping the handle in the slightly heavy-handed way that an actor would, with none of the delicacy that comes from the surgeon's natural trepidation at doing harm. He carves a line down the middle of the body all the way to the pubic hair, swerving to avoid the belly button. This is similar to a laparotomy incision but, instead of blood, bright yellow fat leaps into the crease. In expert sideways sweeps, he moves the knife under the skin of the chest and abdomen, as if peeling fruit. Tissue bends off the underlying muscles and he heaves these open like curtains, the top layer of person revealing a deeper level of human nakedness beneath.

I know he has loads to do before his consultant arrives. But, leisurely on my day off, I feel as if the pathologist travels too quickly over this human terrain. My mind scurries to find familiar things to associate with the odd sights and, by the time I look up again, he's holding a pair of rib shears, which resemble heavy pliers. With breastbone as epicentre, he defines a circle of ribs like a clock face and crunches through them methodically, his knuckles white from the effort. By the time he's done his face is dewy. Then he puts the bone-cutters down and uses a big chisel to prise the sternum up and away from the chest. This makes a ripe plasticky noise, like cling film being ripped from a cardboard roll.

In spite of myself, I turn my face away from the sudden gamey smell as the organs are revealed and, by the time I look again, the pathologist is holding a ladle and plastic measuring jug with notches on its side, like a cook making stock. He reaches into the chest, alongside a lung. I peer in and see the gutter there, red and shiny with pleural fluid, which he carefully ladles into the jug from one side and then another.

After hoicking out both lungs, he begins on the intestine. The surface of the body may be cold as marble, but the viscera retain the supple vibe of life, the gut winding out in loops and endless ribbon-like lengths, thin as fingers, juicy as a mouthful of new gum. With the small bowel in a slippery pile, he begins to winkle the podgy colon out with his hands, burrowing all the way down to the rectum, which he soon produces in his fist. The whole mass is collected in a bowl to prevent it sliding, unruly now that it isn't contained inside the body.

Grabbing a bladeless scalpel handle and moving to the top of the table, the pathologist puts the blunt end through the first incision that he made at the woman's throat. He works the metal handle up and under, releasing the skin from the structures of the face and then creates a gap between the curved bow of the jawbone and its muscles. Last, he reaches for the tongue. The corpse's lips fall open and his gloved hand reappears in her mouth. So this is what the gauntlets are for, to keep the wrists dry! The pathologist strives to free the tongue and his hand soon exits at the base of her neck, bearing its heavy meat in his grip. Using the knife to free the larynx and pharynx, he pulls the mass high above the body. The column of windpipe and oesophagus and aorta rise too until he finally lets the whole rope flop back against her abdomen.

The technician appears again, with an oscillating saw that resembles a pizza cutter with an electric lead. She combs the corpse's hair into a parting from ear to ear, sweeping some forward over the face and the rest backwards, the way men used to with Brylcreem. With the PM40, she carves into this parting, before using both hands to pull the scalp forwards and over the face so that the cut rim of hair sits on the chin as would a beard. The saw roars as she presses it to the skull and a white cloud of bone dust settles in the hair like dandruff. A second cut is made at right angles, where the string of a pair of glasses might sit. With a small chisel, the tech prises a segment of skull from the head, like a quarter of an orange. Underneath is brain, not pulsing as I'm used to seeing it, but very much fresh. I lean in closer, notice the gyral undulations, the tiny cortical vessels.

On the other side of the room, the pathologist is deep in thought. He studies the organs he's arranged along the marble counter, prods them, lifts bits to the light. His boss is due any minute and she will expect a logical, medical analysis, one which culminates in cause of death. The body lies a few feet away, discarded. On the one hand, it's nothing more than a shell, cavernous and rib-slatted as a clinker boat. But it's also the most compelling thing in this room. This was a woman, unmistakable for anyone else. In my mind's eye, I rearrange the corpse's features. Her breasts aren't in the right position anymore, but I appreciate their fullness and imagine whom they might have fed. I look at her fingers, picture them moving and wonder what domestic, professional or loving purposes they served. Hands, feet, face and genitals make a person of her and, by studying them, I start to paint her back into herself.

Nothing thrills me more than the human body. But, until my mid-twenties, it didn't cross my mind someone like me could become a doctor. There were no medics in my family. I was slow at maths and science, and gave them up before the age of sixteen. After school, I decided on an English degree, because it was what I found easiest.

Then, in my final year, something important happened. A few of us were hanging out at a friend's house one evening when his dad, a surgeon from London, arrived to stay for the weekend. Over dinner, we all sat enthralled as he told us stories of his hospital life. But when the plates were cleared and everyone else was about to go out, I realised I had no desire to join them. My friend's dad had offered to fetch a surgical textbook from his bag, full of photos of some of his favourite operations, and I remember sitting at the kitchen table late into the night, poring over these luminous images, skin peeled back to reveal muscle and bone, tumours and blood vessels. It was my first glimpse of real anatomy, and I was astounded by its beauty.

The following year, unhappily employed as a clerical assistant in a publishing house, I heard about a new course being pioneered at one of the big London medical schools. A professor there had developed a hunch. Maybe the usual stock of candidates with perfect science scores weren't the only ones who could make good doctors. What if there was a hidden population of arts students out there, overlooked because they didn't have the right qualifications, who could be trained to do the job just as well?

Before I knew it I had quit my job and was joining nine other unlikely would-be doctors to become the second cohort of the Foundation Course in Natural

Sciences, my single biology O level making me, in that professor's words, the least-qualified medical student in the country. The deal he was offering was tough but miraculous. We would join first-year students of maths, physics, chemistry and biology for their lectures and exams. Anyone able to pass all four subjects at the end of the summer term would get a place at medical school.

The years that followed were some of the happiest of my life. Recognising straightaway that science made more sense to me if I could link it to something personal, I was usually at the hospital, hanging around in someone's operating theatre, on the wards, riding in the back of an ambulance, or visiting the mortuary. And if these experiences occasionally prompted moments of artistic inspiration – a recollection of a phrase of poetry, a philosophical thought, an aesthetic thrill at the sight of the body laid bare in the operating theatre – I simply kept them to myself, subverting my old identity with the will of a would-be scientist determined to pass. It wasn't until years into my training, by which time I was trying to combine a career in surgery with new responsibilities as a mother, that I started to feel some of the constraints as well as the joys of my profession. The more clinical medicine I learned, the less it made sense to me to regard the body as a purely mechanical entity. All too frequently, I saw surgeons disregarding the feelings of their patients. Standing next to my consultant one day while he yanked out staples from a woman's abdomen, showing little consideration for her distress, I found myself thinking back to that radical anatomy professor. Surely, when he was dreaming up a way to bring an arty bunch of kids into the conventional world of medicine, he had something more in mind than simple camouflage? He must have hoped we had something fresh to offer, that we might doctor differently than our more traditional peers?

This book began with a simple desire, to honour the opportunity that professor gave me, to set out on an ecumenical exploration of anatomy, which – by blurring the boundaries that usually separate science from art, rational from emotional, objective from subjective experience – might help me arrive at a deeper and more complete understanding of what we're made of. How wonderful it would be to look at the body through a more human prism, widening the traditional anatomical perspective to include some of my own experiences, pausing occasionally to consider our current medical beliefs within their historical context. I knew I'd find the project hugely enjoyable and imagined it would be straightforward. After all, anatomy has always been a kind of magical hologram to me, this moment Plato-clean, the next drenched in the personal.

But in the middle of writing, serious medical events in my own life changed everything. At precisely the point I might have expected to become intimately in touch with my physical self, I found myself disorientated. Just when I thought being a doctor would be most useful, I felt powerless. When I was finally able to return to writing, I knew that the book had to change, that the detached perspective I had been adopting could only capture part of what I knew to be true. I needed to find a way, alongside the intellectual exploration of the human organs I was in the middle of, to convey something of the messy and frightening experience I now had of living inside a human body, one which had suddenly become a text for other doctors to read.

This book remains an attempt to fulfil my original ambition, to look at anatomy with fresh eyes, approaching the subject more broadly than the humanities and medicine individually allow. It is also my way of grappling with the search itself, of examining what it means to study the human body, and try and know it, at the same time that my own has come under the clinical spotlight. When I set out to write an alternative anatomy, I didn't realise how dramatically my ideas were about to change. When I elected to put myself in the frame, I had no idea how personal this project would become.

September 1995

*We are first-year medical students and testing our new
stethoscopes. My boyfriend's is bright red and stands out
like an artery against his immaculate white coat. We're
by the window in his flat, sun flashing on the river, and
when I lean in, though it's his heart I'm supposed to be
listening to, it's really mine I'm aware of, racing and
skipping the way it sometimes does, especially when I get
this close to him. I try to concentrate but am soon away
again, the nearness of his body, the amplified sound
of his breaths and the clear, strong sound of his heart
tempting me to wonder what might come next, not just
this afternoon, but forever. When it's his turn, he listens
for ages. And his face is so rapt when he looks up that,
for one foolish moment, I expect romance. Instead, he
says, 'I can hear a murmur. There's something wrong
with your heart.'*

Bone

When I was at medical school, we had a stint of pure science at the start of our training, and the anatomy part was especially intense. There were morning lectures to cram our heads with facts, chilly afternoons of cadaveric dissection and continual exams in which – thanks to a system of negative marking – I often scored less than zero. Most challenging though was the impersonal character of these early lessons. Nothing was spiced up with real-life relevance and, for two whole years, we didn't meet a single patient.

It wasn't until I set foot in a hospital that the visceral curiosity which had made me want to be a doctor in the first place flared into life. Suddenly, I saw that knowing what structure went where could mean the difference between saving a life and losing it. Joyfully, I realised that clinical anatomy was going to be as different to what I'd already learned as actually having sex is to what schoolteachers are prepared to tell teenagers about the birds and the bees.

Pushing the doors to an operating theatre open for the first time was like standing in Dorothy's shoes when she walks out of her tornado-transported house into the almost painful, Technicolor clarity of Oz. Beholding a surgeon opening a patient's face as easily as if it were a book, to remove a large tumour, knocked me sideways and I still experience a heightened appreciation of life and beauty whenever I enter this special arena. Decades on, I can't shake the feeling that leaving theatre is like stepping from sunshine into gloom, substituting astounding reality for a faded imitation of what life has on offer. Even now, I sometimes think that meeting a person in normal circumstances, with their skin intact, is a moribund business compared to how it could be if only they were supine on the slab, laid open to display the very best of themselves in the rainbow heaven of the operating theatre, fat a garish custard-yellow, arterial red hitting my retina like a mistake, veins blue under sinuous cover, the ice-white of bone in the deeps.

I never want to return to the bookish pedagogy of those early days. I have a memory from three decades ago, of the first time I saw our ancient professor, wheeling a whole human skeleton into the lecture theatre. I can still picture how beautiful it looked from my seat in the front row, all the tea-coloured bones trembling as he brought it to a standstill. Perhaps it's nostalgia, then, that makes me want to celebrate my first return to the bones in half a lifetime by visiting somewhere grand, to give the skeleton the fervent review it so deserves.

At the Gordon Museum of Pathology in London, somewhere you have to be a doctor or nurse to visit, Bill the curator leads me up the stairs, through serried sparkling galleries each devoted to a different part of the body, until we reach the right section. Then, bountiful as a sommelier, he asks which bones I'd like him to bring. Once he's gone, I look around in wonder. Row upon row of glass jars encase all manner of tumours, fractures and deformities. I could lose myself straightaway, matching pathology specimens with typed excerpts in the leather-bound albums beside them, which give details of who each patient was and how their bodies failed them. But there's a correct order for learning what we're made of. Before disease, it's time to reacquaint myself with the human form in its ideal state.

The skeleton is made of 206 different pieces and, because of this mind-boggling variety, anatomists like to group them. The axial skeleton denotes the bones of the skull and trunk, while the appendicular skeleton means those of the limbs. You'll also hear bones referred to as long, short, flat or sesamoid, this last lovely word describing any piece which develops within a tendon as it crosses a sharp angle in the body. The patella, or kneecap, is a good example.

Labels like these are convenient, but the real beauty of the skeleton is expressed in its diversity, the perfect way each unit marries form and function. Peering into the glass case here, it's clear that the skull's main job is to protect the brain. Look how the thick cranial plates interleave snugly around where this most precious organ would once have rested. Glance at the wide bowl of the female pelvis and your eyes are drawn straight to the outlet, the gaping hole in its centre through which a baby passes before taking its first breath. Imagine putting the ribs in order of size to fashion a bony cage, and marvel at how something so delicate is able to protect our heart and lungs from assault. Compare the massive levers of the arms and legs. Or picture the carpal bones of the hand in your own palm, like a collection of marbles, and try to solve the riddle of putting them in order.

Bill is back in no time, depositing two containers on the table in front of me. One is big, the other neat as a jewellery box, and I flip open its lid to find the tiniest bone in the human body sitting on a little cushion inside. Weighing just six milligrams, titchier than a child's fingernail, the stapes nonetheless has star status in my own specialty of ear, nose and throat surgery, as one of the three ossicles in the middle ear that enable us to hear. I place the stirrup in the palm of my hand and wonder what tender and sorrowful words it once conveyed to its owner, imagine sound waves entering their ear canal, reaching the eardrum and making it vibrate. I think of how these waves would then have travelled from malleus, to incus, to stapes before passing to the inner ear. I look at the white splinter in my hand and am amazed to think of it once upon a time rocking and transmitting information through the cochlea, all the way to the owner's brain, to be read as sound and turned into meaning there.

I lay the stapes carefully back in its box and then turn to the big container, hauling off its lid. Inside lies a treasure trove of femurs, criss-crossed like sticks in a bonfire. The thigh bones differ in length, thickness, weight, colour and state of preservation. I marvel at the size and shape of this cartoonish, bone-shaped bone, the biggest in the body, which articulates with the acetabulum of the hip bone above and the condyles of the tibia and the back of the patella below.

Why are we so ready to squander pleasure in the way we teach anatomy? I pick up a femur and simply hold it. I run my hand along the sweep of its shaft as protectively as a cheerleader would on her baton, enjoying the contrast between its overall smooth finish and the ridged linea aspera on its posterior surface where the chunky muscles of the thigh attach. I notice the sound it makes as I place it on the wooden table as if it too were made of sanded wood. With the common language used for all long bones, I identify the thin bit in the middle as the diaphysis, the round nobble at each end the epiphysis and the crucial transition between the two – which contains the growth plate – the metaphysis. I open the anatomy book I've brought with me to remind me of the nitty-gritty.

The big bump at the end of the femur, which looks like a snowy outcrop, is the greater trochanter, the point of attachment to the most solid of our butt muscles, the gluteus maximus. The beautiful globe is the femoral head and I can't resist slotting my little finger into its fovea, the dimple which usually houses the thick ligament that connects the ball of the femur to the socket of the hip bone. I remember my childhood dolly, whose plastic limbs and head were secretly attached to her peachy rubber trunk by tight elastic bands. And the unforgettable sight of her blonde head rolling down the pavement after my brother accidentally snapped it off by tugging her from me. I finger the daintiness of the neck of the femur, the place that breaks so easily in old ladies when their bones get thin, the injury recognisable by the sickening sight of the abnormally shortened, out-turned leg. I observe the tiny holes in the diaphysis, where blood vessels would have penetrated the bone, supplying oxygen to all of its cells. I flip the femur over and inspect the other end, where two roughened epicondyles form the flare of the diaphysis and the twinned knobbly condyles at the back curve out to greet the bones of the lower limb at the knee joint.

The femur is close to my face now and I notice where a chip has come off the greater trochanter. The resulting defect is tiny but, through it, I can decipher the two main layers that all bones are made of, the outer cortex and the inner medulla. Cortical bone makes up eighty per cent of an adult's overall skeleton, which is surprising because it seems a paltry layer in a single example like this, as if the bone had been dipped in paint, or stingily covered in icing. The medullary bone below is quite different in appearance, with holes called trabeculae as plain to see as those in a Crunchie bar. Children's bones consist mainly of this lighter material, whereas adults only have a small amount of it left, enough to store precious marrow and ensure our bones aren't too heavy to lug about.

But then I stop short. I won't get far like this. I can

only elucidate a fraction of the true geography of bone by looking into the broken tip of this old femur. And not on account of the limited view, but because an ancient relic can't provide more than an inkling of what real bones are like. I think of the Greek word *skeletos*, which means 'dried out' and so perfectly depicts the desiccated, inanimate way we doctors are trained to think not just about the bones but the body as a whole. And, suddenly it's clear to me: dead anatomy is false anatomy.

So, banish whatever associations you might have formed between the skeleton and death. Jolly Rogers and bird carcasses picked clean. Catacombs and dinosaur fossils. The Grim Reaper, fleshless beneath his cloak, and ashes scattered on the sea. Bone is alive. The bones inside your body may have the same basic shape as the bits of skeleton I've been looking at here, but their essence is different. Live bones aren't the same as the ones I've got spread out in front of me, or those you've seen in your biology lab, or the grand bones at the Natural History Museum, unearthed in an archae-ological dig. Compared to the bones inside your body right now, those others are nothing more than ghosts.

Imagine instead this sunshiny view. You are inside a living person's leg and, like the 1970s Six Million Dollar Man, you can see – with microscopic clarity – right down to the most basic building blocks of their femur. Straight up, what you'll notice is that the rim of outer cortex which covers the bone isn't some inert shell after all. Its job is to stop the bone breaking under the physical stresses of everyday life and, to do that, it has to be purposeful and alive. Zoom in on a thumbprint-sized stretch of cortex, and you'll find it's made of thousands of identical units called osteons, which run parallel to the long axis of the bone. Cut one of them across like a small felled tree, and marvel at how the concentric layers, each rich with collagen and mineral salts, run at right angles to those on either side, maximising tensile strength. Spy what's known as the Haversian canal running through the osteons' centre, which is teeming with arteries, veins, lymphatics and nerves to keep it vital. Observe the horizontally placed Volkmann's canals, which enable all the Haversian canals to communicate with each other, apart from at the outermost edge, where a protective flexible sheath called the periosteum covers each bone as a falconer's glove does her hand.

Now burrow down to the medulla. In a dead bone, what we were looking at had the appearance of hardened sponge. But cut across a real bone and the first thing you notice is how succulent its centre is. Bones aren't just punctured here and there by blood vessels; their core is packed full of bone marrow. Red marrow is plush with stem cells, from which over 200 billion red and white blood cells are made each day. This is gradually replaced by yellow marrow, which is a great fat store, so that the only remaining red stuff we have as adults is found in our hips, ribs, spine, chest and the ends of our long bones.

If I had to prepare for an exam, these osteological facts would press themselves on me like the wrong kind of kiss. But when I dream at the same time as learning, I feel nothing but pleasure. I could stand forever in this well of sunshine in the Gordon Museum, in the cosy solitude of anatomical musing. I could ask Bill to show me everything he's got, bring me box after box, scrutinise every single fragment of the human skeleton in turn and, as long as I was able to mix facts with reverie, to let the poetry of the body whistle through its infinite spaces, I'd never grow tired. But what about my own bones? If someone stumbled across my remains in the future, what might they reveal?

With the help of the CRANID skull database, a physical anthropologist would place me in one of eight broad ethnogeographic groups. From the general state of my skeleton, the lack of stress markers like Harris lines in the tibia, it would be clear I've escaped nasty childhood disease and have been well fed. My sex would declare itself in my pelvis, with its greater subpubic angle, broad sciatic notch and preauricular sulcus. My age would be easy to guess too since, just past my mid-century, all my epiphyses would be fused. There would be some degeneration, early signs of osteopenia and perhaps some tattiness where my ribs meet the side of the sternum. Who knows, there might even be a little osteoarthritis, narrowing of the joint spaces, and rough outcrops of bone called osteophytes protruding from my hip and knee joints. But there are limits to what even an expert can read in the text of someone's bones. They may get as far as detecting scars from old injuries, but would remain blind to the paradoxically banal significance of the events which caused them.

Nasal fracture. It's halcyon midsummer. I am eight years old and swimming in a neighbour's pool. Each time I come up, there is a spangling of colour and sound: luminous green grass and trees, a high white sky freckled with birds, towels baking on yellow chairs, laughter and the voice of an adult calling my younger brother and me for lunch. I don't obey then and there, because I'm experimenting with something important, how I can separate joy into spaces, up and out or down and in. I can pierce the surface of the water and join the happy clamour, or sink instead into the dream of a deeper blue self. Kneeling by the metal filter, I test the limits of my breath before pressing my feet hard against the bottom of the pool and thrusting myself up. As I break the varnished lid of water, my face tilts skywards for relief and, at this exact moment, seeing only flat blue, my brother throws a heavy toy across the pool. There is a sharp crack as our two trajectories intersect and blood runs through the water like dye.

What else is there in my personal catalogue of bone? An avulsion fracture of the right ankle from jumping off a rock in Egypt and landing awkwardly, a stress fracture of the tibia from too much running as a young woman. The mishaps of my own children, whose bones are dearer to me than my own: my son's fractured foot from tumbling off a top bunk and broken nose from careening down a sand dune; my eldest girl's right fractured radius after slipping off a climbing frame in rain-wet shoes and – ten years later – her own broken nose from running into a glass door at a teenage party; a twin's dislocated elbow from falling while holding her sister's hand. What makes these breaks inconsequential is the fact that the skeleton, the part of our body we think of as being most solid, is constantly shape-shifting. To see how this works, blur your gaze a little, until all the different fragments merge into a whole. Imagine the skeleton melted into a single pot of bone.

Babies aren't born with a formed skeleton, perfectly shaped and fit for purpose like a set of Meccano. Instead, during foetal life, a basic template of cartilage and fibrous tissue is laid down. This stage is like the line drawing in a colouring book, before someone has filled it in with felt-tips. The transformation of the shadow skeleton is called ossification. First, a tough material called osteoid replaces the template skeleton and then mineral salts are deposited into the scaffolding, making hard bone. In most short bones, this happens from one central hub called an ossification centre. Long bones are more complicated. They have a primary ossification centre in the diaphysis, but also two secondary ossification centres, one within each metaphysis, where lengthening of the bone continues into young adulthood, from a highly active strip of cartilage called the growth plate. The skull has several such hubs, suture lines forming where bone from adjacent centres meet, leaving soft spaces called fontanelles that you can feel disconcertingly in a baby's head until the plates of hard bone are completely developed.

Ossification is higgledy-piggledy across the body and even within individual sites. Take the humerus, the elegant bone of your upper arm. The diaphysis appears in utero at about eight weeks. At the shoulder end, the two knobbly bits of humerus, which are known as the greater and lesser trochanter, ossify at one to two years and four to five years respectively. But, even then, they don't join up with the shaft until a person is between eighteen and twenty-one, just when that youthful arm is lifting its first legal drink. At the lower end of the humerus, the other two knobbly bits, the medial and lateral epicondyles, form at four to six and twelve years respectively, connecting to the shaft at fourteen to sixteen. This continues throughout the human skeleton, with the fusing of the 360 bone fragments we're born with into the 206 bones we consider the adult standard not wrapped up until we are about thirty years old.

Even after our foundation skeleton is established, there's nothing static about it. The skeleton that supports you now literally didn't exist a decade ago. Every year, about ten per cent of your bone is replaced, always dissolving, always rebuilding. This happens to repair injuries, cracks and deformities as we go about the hazardous business of living, to thin down or bulk up individual bones in response to their daily load, and to supply our bloodstream with the exact levels of the minerals calcium and phosphate that are essential for so many of the body's other functions.

Two main types of bone cell collaborate in this remodelling, all of them starting out as stem cells in the bone marrow. Osteoclasts are called in when a piece of bone needs to be refashioned. This might be in the growing skeleton of a child, or at a site of injury, or just in a section that hasn't been replaced for a while and is becoming decrepit. Once at their destination, osteoclasts fasten onto the bone and seal it off like roadworks. Next, they release acid and enzymes, which make a tiny hole, ripe for the next team of cells to do their bit.

Osteoblasts make new bone. Attracted to the gaps, they set about filling them by secreting orderly layers of osteoid, which they then scatter with calcium and phosphate salts, which harden into the mineralised substance we call bone. This takes three to four months. Osteoblasts finish their life by becoming osteocytes, which are by far the commonest bone cells.

Before leaving the Gordon Museum, I take one last look inside the box of femurs. I wonder to whom they might have belonged, this one a small child, that thick one perhaps to a working man, its girth suggesting the erstwhile attachment of bulky muscles? I reflect on how each person's story is written in their bones. Idly, I lay the last femur on top of my summer dress, in the correct anatomical position. Was this once a woman's thigh? What kind of life did she have? I cross my leg and uncross it again, watching the femur move in line with my own.

Have you noticed a person's flaws are the flip side of their strengths? The same is true of bone where, fractures aside, most serious disease occurs as a consequence of its sheer dynamism, something going awry with the balance between formation and dissolution. The most common example is osteopenia, the thinning of bone which happens to perimenopausal women like me, when falling oestrogen levels cause more to be lost than can be replaced. This results in an attrition rate of ten per cent of bone mass per decade and, ultimately, osteoporosis. On the flip side, excessive bone deposition is seen in conditions like Paget's disease, fibrodysplasia and osteopetrosis. And in a rare but devastating disease called osteogenesis imperfecta, a failure of osteoblasts to make the essential collagen component of good osteoid leads to repeated fractures and even death.

Even the tiny stapes can be put out of action by something called otosclerosis, the leading cause of deafness in young people. Because the ossicles of the ear are so intricate, remodelling here is meant to be held in check by a protein called osteoprotegerin. In this disease, though, the tight control system fails:

osteoclastic resorption is followed by osteoblastic over-activity, so that the stapes becomes fixed. Because the chain of ossicles can't rock against each other as they're meant to, sound conduction is impaired. The best treatment is a very fiddly operation called stapedec-tomy, which involves removing the encrusted stapes, and replacing it with a plastic or wire substitute.

Undoubtedly, though, the most pathologically dynamic disease process to affect the human skeleton is cancer. Bone malignancy is usually secondary, a tumour from elsewhere eventually spreading to sites such as the pelvis and spine, but there is a rare and dev-astating type which starts out in bone itself. In a situation like this, even a great surgeon may have to adjust their usual heroic ambitions.

The Royal National Orthopaedic Hospital, Stanmore, centre of excellence for all things bone. I am standing in front of an X-ray screen, while one of the senior consultants, Mr P, puts up an image of a thigh, the soft grey tissue casting into relief the white of bone. At the top, near the pelvis, he points to the sunburst sign, where abnormal tissue appears to explode out from the medulla of the femur, through the cortex and periosteum. During my time working in emer-gency medicine, I learned to recognise the dark line on an X-ray that indicated a bone had been broken. I also know what arthritic hips and knees look like, and even the blotchy appearance of metastatic cancer. I have never seen anything like this. He explains that most of the bone tumours referred to him are chondrosarcomas, osteosarcomas and Ewing's sarcomas. You can tell this woman – he gestures to the person asleep on the operating table – is from the first group because she still has her hair. Osteosarcoma patients get chemotherapy before their operations, but chondosarcomas aren't sensitive to drugs, so these patients go straight to surgery.

Across the room, the patient is covered in drapes from head to toe, apart from her left leg which sticks out almost casually from the sarcophagus of green, like a leg thrust free from under a bedsheet on a hot holiday night. For sterility, her foot is tucked into a surgical glove, while the rest of her leg is painted brown with betadine, streaky as bottle tan.

Mr P measures on the computer where the tumour sits in relation to normal landmarks on the femur. He picks up a steel ruler and purple pen and, at the sleeping woman's bedside, draws a line from the feminine curve of her hip all the way along one side of her leg to the ankle bone, before cross-hatching this seam. Then, applying his steel ruler, he matches the data he has gleaned from looking at the X-ray to the body in front of him. In segments, from the curved outpost of the greater trochanter, he moves the ruler down, adding length after length until he reaches a point where he draws a clear horizontal line across the vertical one. Here he writes the letters TP to indicate the transection point, where he intends to cut across the femur.

After scrubbing, Mr P traces his knife along the length of the woman's thigh with the lightness of a caress. Dissecting open skin and fat with the hot wand of cutting diathermy, he zaps little bleeding vessels as he goes. Then he works through the tough tendon of gluteus maximus, right down to the perfect ball of the femoral head, which gleams with cartilage like a huge silver marble. He has entered the zone all surgeons must, the mechanical obliterating the personal. By contrast, as a pure observer, I have the luxury of flipping between perspectives: she is a woman, she is tissue. He lifts the leg, grasping around the ankle and moving it this way and that, to loosen the thigh in relation to the hip bone. He uses blunt dissection, hooking fingers of muscle up, and cutting down onto his glove with the diathermy. The tumour is on the outside of the hip joint but damn close to it, running all the way up to the groin. It becomes tricky to reach. And, as he is leaning in, the disease-frail femur breaks.

There is now no choice but to cut the thigh bone across, leaving enough of a stump of bone at its lower end to attach a prosthesis. Mr P holds an electric saw but, even though this makes for lighter work than an old-fashioned tool, he still has to bear down on it, pressing into the bone, a small cloud of white dust accompanying the loud mosquito whine. The femur is cut through like the trunk of a tree, forest work. And, like a lumberjack, while he must expect the sudden collapse that comes from getting all the way through, he still falls forward just a little and exhales.

Suddenly, I am looking at a cross-section of the biggest bone in the body. The great circle of it is as bright and round as a moon. The outer yellow-white rim is a few millimetres thick. Within this ring, the bone is textured and a rich purple. Marrow saturates the trabeculae. The core of the femur is briskly bleeding. It looks soft as a sponge but, when the registrar holds the end of his suction tube to it intermittently to deal with the blood that pools repeatedly on its round surface, you can see that what the sucker rests against is solid. This spectacular bone is alive. It is not dust. It does not whisper from the past. It is the truth of one person laid flat, life and limb no longer salvageable, tumour fisting, abnormal blood supply like wrinkled witchy fingers, cancer now seeded from thigh to lung, to take this woman to her grave, surely before this year is out, before the sunshine slamming on the pavement outside is replaced by frost.

The whole cut section of thigh bone is lifted up and out of the leg. Because it is still sheathed in tissue, it doesn't look like a bone but more like a skinny little leg being removed from a bigger leg. The remaining stump of femur is drilled clean of its yellow marrow. Green 'trials', like golf balls, are slotted into the hip socket until the right size is found. Purple-blue trial shafts are also fitted and then both are swapped for the 'definitive', which is a titanium ball and rod. A mesh called a Trevira sleeve is pulled over the rod, like a sock, before bone cement is squirted snugly into the drilled-out femur. The prosthesis is pressed into position at the hip and knee end, and all the muscles are sewed correctly back in place.

I look at the young woman's body as the bloodied drapes are removed; the shape of her reminds me of myself. Mr P tells me the tumour is as aggressive as it gets. It has probably grown from abnormal cartilage cells at the growth plate of the femur, and wouldn't have been there even six months ago. He lugs the specimen, which is as big as one of my forearms, a tumour the size of a fist attached to one side of it, into a bucket. And it's only when he adds that he never would have imagined, as a junior surgeon, that some of the most satisfying operations he'd end up doing would be palliative, that the penny drops. Mr P has spent five hours reinforcing his patient's disease-weakened leg, to prevent an excruciating spontaneous fracture. He was never going to be able to save her life.

When I was at medical school, I was given a box of bones to take home. The size of a small coffin, it sat in my bedroom next to my desk. When I first emptied it out on the floor, it took me a while to realise that I had been given only a half-skeleton. There was a skull, spine, sternum and pelvis, but all the paired bones of the chest and limbs were singly represented. I've learned since then that most of these skeletons were shipped over to UK medical schools from India, where bone farmers were paid derisory amounts to deflesh and bleach human remains for our delectation. At the time, though, I felt conned. I suppose I'd hoped my skeleton would be complete like the one in the lecture on that exciting first morning, so that I could hang it in my sitting room, play ghoulish with it, show it off to my non-medical friends.

What an ass I was. I'm ashamed I didn't feel the poetry of those bones back then, what a privilege it was to look after them for a couple of years. As a middle-aged woman who feels death lurking at every corner, I know exactly what I would say now, if it were my job to hand out these precious boxes to a room full of callow newbie medics. You have been given half-skeletons for more than reasons of economy. We can teach you an osteological vocabulary, we can help you find your way around every fragment of the human skeleton. We can show you why the bones have the contours they do, what other structures pass alongside and through them, what protection they give to the softer organs they encase. But all this is only part of the picture. The rest is personal, and you have to discover it for yourself. Go to the Emergency Room, observe quietly in an operating theatre, visit an orthopaedic clinic. Stand in the mirror and hunt for your own bony prominences. Examine ancient faces. Be like the fabulous Jacobean John Webster and look for the skull beneath the skin.

After all, bones aren't just a doctor's ken. My parents got me and my brothers together recently. Keen to spare us a tricky decision in the future, they asked what we thought should happen to their bodies when they die. I said I favoured cremation, for its convenience. But one of my brothers felt differently and soon persuaded them to keep the plot they have reserved in the local graveyard. I am so glad now that he did. If my mum and dad are lucky enough to leave the final document of their skeletons intact, the last thing I'd want to do is destroy them. I too would like them to be buried. Somewhere my siblings and I, and all of our children, can visit them and feel the weight of their bones beneath our feet.

Genitals

The bodies we learned about at medical school always belonged to someone else. Thinking or talking about our own would have seemed inappropriate, like interfering with the purity of science. But insisting on this separation of the academic and the subjective doesn't make sense to me. A doctor's first knowledge of anatomy, like anyone's, comes from personal experience.

A poster on the wall of my primary school classroom depicts a girl's stepwise progress into womanhood. She must be me. On the left of the chart, I find my likeness, a slim-hipped pelvis with its familiar internal staghorn shape of womb, ovaries and fallopian tubes. The politest of smiles between the legs. Tracking right, I confront my destiny, as outlandish as the planets on the neighbouring poster. There's no escape: one day, I will morph into that heavy-hipped, full-breasted woman, the secrets of her genitals overlayed by a wide forest of hair.

Back home, a gang of baby-girl dolls in the cot at the foot of my bed help me arrive at a piecemeal knowledge. Some have a faint groove etched in the curve of their crotch. In others, this has been neglected in favour of a purely urological interpretation of the vagina, a perfect tiny hole through which the water I feed them empties to wet their nappy.

In a strip-lit loo cubicle at boarding school, I try to fathom the diagram meant to help me insert my first tampon, a sagittal section through a female's innards, coloured in blue to distract from the inescapably red project. I have no idea of how to angle the cardboard applicator to achieve open-sesame, and feel nauseated by the half-numb arrival of the dense swab into what feels like nowhere, leaving me only a string to pull on for reassurance. Years of periods follow, in which I discover that my vagina will turn against me every month, not giving me any helpful bladder-like warning but leaking unannounced, a crimson violence left wherever I sit.

What else? Adolescent boys' fingers, unwashed and untutored, trying their best to reciprocate against the tide of their own delight; the cold specula of smear-tests. But hang on a minute. Why only this mechanical litany? How about the carnal fun that played such a central part in my puberty? Where is that lusty girl I know I was? Here's the thing. These snapshots may be skewed, but if I narrow the frame to just those memories that involve the vagina, only the joyless, functional ones get included.

The anatomy of the genitals needs a rewrite. Rip out the textbook pages which silo the penis and vagina in their own lonely chapters. Delete those sections from your screens. Everything I was taught about this part of our bodies was premised on a false opposition. But before I can explode some of the received wisdom, I need to acquaint you with it. So, for better or worse, here are the nuts and bolts of what I was taught at medical school.

Whether you become male or female – we were told – is written in your genes. Most human cells contain a person's genetic information in their nucleus, arranged along twenty-three pairs of chromosomes. Half of each pair is inherited from our biological father and half from our mother. The last set is different from all the others. These are sex chromosomes, where our reproductive and genital destiny is written. Our mother always donates an X chromosome to this pair, while our father gives either an X or a Y. If the resulting combination is XY, we are born with a penis. If the combination is XX, we are born with a vagina. The only cells that don't have the full quota of DNA are sperm and eggs which carry just their own half.

At five weeks' gestation, tiny swellings called genital ridges appear and germ cells, which will one day become either sperm or eggs, migrate there. By six to eight weeks, the reproductive system consists of two primitive gonads, sitting next to two structures called the Mullerian and Wolffian ducts. All human embryos have the same future reproductive equipment at this stage. What happens next depends on that all-important pair of sex chromosomes.

The Y chromosome contains a segment called the SRY, which stands for 'sex-determining region of the Y chromosome'. If an embryo is XY, the SRY produces a protein called 'testis-determining factor' at eight weeks' gestation, and the previously ambi-sexual gonads are prompted to become testes. Testes then make two hormones which push the process on to the next level. The first is testosterone, which triggers Wolffian ducts to turn into male reproductive struc-tures, such as the epididymis, vas deferens and seminal vesicles. The second is anti-Mullerian hormone, which makes the Mullerian ducts degenerate, so that female reproductive parts can't form.

According to this paradigm, the default position for all embryos is female. If there is no Y chromosome and therefore no SRY region, the absence of testis-determining factor means that Wolffian ducts wither.

Equally, the absence of anti-Mullerian hormone causes the Mullerian duct system to develop into female reproductive structures, for example the upper vagina, ovaries, fallopian tubes and uterus.

By ten weeks' gestation, an internal reproductive pattern has emerged, along what are conventionally considered male or female lines. This is known as sex determination. Somewhat confusingly, the completely separate process by which sex determination translates into the formation of fleshy genitals is called sexual differentiation. But before I go there, I want to stop and put the kibosh on the certainty of what I've laid out so far. Because the reality is that the genetics of sex are as clear as mud.

For starters, the idea that the presence or absence of a Y chromosome dictates sex is vastly simplistic. People with intersex conditions, also known as Differences of Sexual Development (DSDs), disrupt this neat taxonomy in that while their chromosomes say one thing, their gonads or sexual anatomy say another. These individuals are usually divided into two groups. The first are those with missing or extra chromosomes, such as females with Turner syndrome who are XO, or males with Klinefelter syndrome who are XXY. The second group either can't make or respond to sex hormones in the usual way. But this isn't all.

Researchers have identified more than twenty-five genes involved in DSDs, and advances in gene sequencing have unveiled a wide spectrum of variations in these genes, each exerting its own effects. An endocrinology paper published in *Nature* in 2014 suggests up to one in a hundred of us may have some form of DSD.

The belief that femaleness is the passive default option, and that the SRY region alone confers maleness, has also been toppled. The recent discovery of genes like WNT4, which actively promotes the ovarian and suppresses the testicular programme, makes it likely that the identity of the gonad is determined by a much more nuanced contest between two opposing networks of gene activity. It turns out that there are very few characteristics solely controlled by the presence or absence of the Y chromosome.

But that's not all. Sex can vary even at a cellular level. In 2010, Paul James, an Australian clinical geneticist, was performing amniocentesis – a routine procedure used for prenatal diagnosis – on a pregnant woman, when he discovered that half of her cells carried two X chromosomes and the other half an X and a Y. He deduced she must have started out as a twin in her own mother's womb, her embryonic cells mingling with those of a deceased sibling she never knew existed.

There are other examples too. In genetic mosaicism,

an individual develops from a single fertilised egg but, due to an error in how the body's cells divide as the embryo is forming, ends up with a patchwork of cells with slightly different genetics. And in micro-chimaerism, stem cells cross the placenta. In 2012, immunologist Lee Nelson from Seattle wowed the scientific community when she described having found XY cells in post-mortem samples of women's brains who had once been pregnant with a boy. It turns out that these rogue cells aren't passive but integrate into and perform special functions in their new environment. Some scientists now feel that the only rational way we can look at sex is on a cell-by-cell basis, seeing each as driven by a complex interplay of different molecular interactions.

Discussing sexual identity can feel treacherous. But it wasn't always so. In the nineteenth century, scientists were quite comfortable with the notion that sex can be arranged in a multiplicity of ways, because their main area of study was the animal kingdom. And while most mammals and birds have a system similar to ours, ending up male or female depending on whether the mother adds a W or Z chromosome to the Z always donated by the father, plenty of other species arrive at sex by mechanisms that have nothing to do with genetics. Painted turtles get their sex according to the

temperature of the nest at a key point of egg incuba-
tion, cold conditions making males and vice versa.
Green spoonworm sex is arrived at by location – those
who fall on the open seabed become female, whereas
those who happen to land on top of a female become
male. Clownfish all start out male, but can flip sex later
on if called upon to replace a dominant female in the
group who has died. Sexual identity among whiptail
lizards is a slam dunk, as they are always female.

According to Sarah Richardson's book *Sex Itself:
The Search for Male and Female in the Human Genome*,
views about sex determination only started to narrow
as a result of specific historical events. Around the
turn of the twentieth century, microscopes became
powerful enough for scientists to scrutinise cells for
the first time. In 1891, the German cytologist Hermann
Henking spotted what would later be called the X
chromosome in the sperm of a fire wasp and, by the
1920s and 30s, the idea of strict biological sex gained
real traction as genetic science cohered with the discovery of male and female sex hormones. It's amazing
to think the infamous SRY region wasn't identified
until 1990. Just a few decades later, its once tight reign
is looking decidedly shaky.

This type of science can feel pretty abstruse. And
you might take the view that, in the arena of sex and

gender, you'd rather keep your head down. But I don't know a soul who's not interested in their own genitals, so come back on familiar ground. I'm about to show you that, even here, in the supposedly safe domain of your own private anatomy, things are more wonderful than they seem.

There's no ignoring the cock and balls. Encased in a capsule called the tunica albuginea, the testes weigh twenty-five grams each and are divided into hundreds of wedge-shaped lobes. These are packed with coils called seminiferous tubules, which contain Sertoli cells, where sperm is made. Dotted around the tubules are testosterone-producing Leydig cells.

Sperm travels from the testis to a two-week holding pen called the epididymis, before moving, by peristalsis, into a tube called the vas deferens. Each vas receives seminal fluid from the seminal vesicles along its way, an alkaline substance whose job is to neutralise the acidic vagina and supply sperm with fructose for fuel. Once past the landmark of the seminal vesicles, the paired vasa deferentia are renamed ejaculatory ducts. Before joining the urethra, they pass through the prostate gland and past the bulbourethral glands, which add lubricant.

Sitting proudly in front of the testes, in glorious

limelight, is the penis. This male organ, used alternately for peeing and ejaculation, is divided into three parts. The root is hidden inside the body and attached to the pelvis by two strong ligaments. It comprises three columns of erectile tissues, two crura and a bulb, all covered by muscles called ischiocavernosus and bulbospongiosus. The second part of the penis, which its owner gazes down on from above, is the shaft or body and is a continuation of the tissues of the root, renamed as they come into view. What were the crura on the inside become two corpora cavernosa on the outside, spongy columns of tissue which each contain a fat artery and become stiff with blood, forming that almost flat upper surface of the penis when it is erect. Nestled underneath is the corpus spongiosus, the continuation of the bulb of the penis, which also fills with blood during arousal, though less so, since it contains the urethra, which needs not to get squashed during ejaculation. All three columns are individually enclosed by the tunica albuginea. The third part of the penis is the tip or glans. An extension of the corpus spongiosus, this is where the urethra exits. Densely packed with nerve endings, it is covered with a bit of skin called the prepuce or foreskin.

I've already explained that female and male gonads

develop identically to start with. Ovaries have the same basic function as testes, which is to produce gametes and sex hormones. About the size of a large grape, each is surrounded by the tunica albuginea and attached to the posterior surface of the broad ligament of the uterus. Ovaries have an outer cortex and inner medulla, and the former is laden with ovarian follicles, inside each of which an oocyte forms. Between 1 and 2 million are created when a female is a foetus in her mother's womb, and the development of these eggs is then suspended until a female child reaches puberty. At this point, hormones prompt eggs to mature, a single one usually being released every month until menopause.

But here is where democracy ends. At this important juncture in our mapping of female reproductive anatomy, we completely lose our way. For what are we girls and women taught is our equivalent to the show-grabbing and flamboyant penis? The vagina. Well, I want to say this upfront. We have been sold a dud. The vagina is a con. Let me explain why. Of course the vagina exists. It is the tubular space that connects the female genitalia to the womb. Actually, to be accurate, it is what is known anatomically as a 'potential space' since, most of time, it is held shut by the ischiocavernosus muscle. But space is all the vagina is. It's like a distraction technique, a portal that comes into play only when something passes through it: a finger or penis, tampon or contraceptive device going in, menstrual blood or a baby coming out. At best, the vagina is a conduit, at worst an absence, a lacuna, a downright anatomical black hole.

Claiming the vagina is the equivalent of the penis is plain wrong. I'll expand on this in a moment, but first want to stress that our disregard for the truth about female genitalia underlies some major problems. According to the WHO, there are 200 million girls and women alive today who have suffered female genital mutilation. Labiaplasty surgery – a cosmetic operation in which the adult vulva is nipped and tucked to look more like a child's – is one of the fastest-growing cosmetic procedures in the world, while gender identity services remain pitifully underfunded. In the US, access to abortion is more restricted than it's been in decades, yet the website Goop is free to promulgate nonsense advising women to steam and insert jade eggs into their vaginas. In the UK, a 2019 YouGov survey revealed that half of Britons can't even label or describe the female genitalia. But there are more subtle costs to our ignorance too.

If we girls and women are led to believe our genitals are a blank, what hope do we have? How can we begin to situate our experience and our desire? No wonder, when we are told that the vagina is what we have instead of the penis, that we get so confused, that the way we feel about our most private selves is so provisional, so banked up on the needs of others. If we are educated that the focus of our genital anatomy is an absence, it's no mystery that our understanding of, and language for, what we feel between our legs ranges from perfunctory to non-existent. No wonder we are on the back foot, somehow imagining that our appetites are essentially passive, that we can't hope for more than the satisfaction of being filled. No shit that we aren't sure what we want, that we are unclear about whether to say yes or no. That we are spectators, not questers. Because, for desire to exist, we need an anatomy of desire, candid information that might allow us to point, gesture and push ourselves forward. In her book *Promiscuities*, Naomi Wolf argues that women need to start documenting their subjective genital experiences. She calls this writing the first-person sexual. But how can we begin to do this accurately when the semiotics we are taught, from when we are knee-high to grasshoppers, all the way into womanhood, say our genitals essentially don't exist? That compared to the magnificent, bouncy, spunking penis, what we have between our legs is little more than a gap?

The vagina may provide a warm, sexy home for the penis but the two are far from equivalent. The truth is much more exciting and radically different to the version we've all inherited. But to get there, we're going to need some help from an oft-neglected part of medicine.

Embryology is the ancient history of the body. It tells us about the origins of the organs. It tracks the serpentine journey our tissues take before ending up in their final arrangement. The most thorough recent embryological investigation into this area is Dylan Isaacson's 2018 study, which looked at the genitals of eighty foetuses ranging between six and twenty-four weeks' gestation, using optical projection tomography, light-sheet fluoresecence microscopy and scanning electron microscopy. It is an excellent place to go for the detail.

While genetics determine whether our gonads become testes or ovaries, sexual differentiation – what happens to our external genitalia – is entirely decided by hormones, specifically the presence or absence of androgens. Until three months of foetal gestation, all genitals are exactly the same. After that, in the male embryo, where testes have developed, the key hormone driving the emergence of male genitalia is an offshoot of testosterone called dihydrotestosterone.

In the female embryo, where ovaries have developed, the key hormone driving the formation of the female external genitalia is a type of oestrogen called oestradiol. But here's the crux. This is what I want my kids to know. Even when male and female genitals do start to diverge, the differences between them remain tiny. And, within what is essentially a very similar anatomical scheme, the equivalent of the penis isn't the vagina, but the clitoris.

In both sexes, the common origin – the unformed lump of clay, so to speak – is a nub of tissue called the genital tubercle. At about twelve weeks, this starts to enlarge at the top of the perineum. In the male, it grows out at a ninety-degree angle to become the glans penis. In the female, the genital tubercle becomes the glans clitoris, hugging the body more closely but achieving the same size between twelve and thirteen weeks. Because even the adult clitoris is tethered against the pubic bone by a deep suspensory ligament, and the majority of its boomerang-shaped form remains hidden within the soft tissue of the perineum, the glans is the only bit that's visible, and this has led to the long-held fallacy that it is a diminutive structure. In fact, the clitoris is a substantial organ, with all the same component parts as the penis.

Embryology is enlightening here, too. At about thirteen weeks' gestation, the glans of the penis and the clitoris fuse with the shaft. In both sexes, this structure contains the exact same three columns of erectile tissue – two corpora cavernosa and a corpus spongiosus. The way these columns of tissue extend into the root is also the same. Reflecting male anatomy, the clitoral corpora cavernosa become paired five-to-nine-centimetre crura, highly erectile bits of tissue which fan out on each side and are attached by ligaments to the pelvis, while vestibular bulbs, just like the bulb of the penis, reach down to form the side walls of the vagina, as well as hugging the lowermost part of the urethra.

Peripheral parts of the male and female perineum are also mirror images. While bulbourethral glands – also called Cowper's glands – form in the male, greater vestibular glands – also known as Bartholin's glands – pop up from exactly the same embryological tissue in the female, secreting the genital wetness that is the happy facilitator of sex. The epithelial buds which become the male prostate, form the female para-urethral glands of Skene, which make a fluid thought to have lubricant and antibacterial properties. Labio-scrotal swellings develop into the male scrotum, while staying unfused as the labia majora in women. And the

pelvic floor muscles ischiocavernosus and bulbospongiosus are identical in either sex.

Even the blood vessels and nerves are alike, and
while many doctors might be able to tell you about
the former – that the arterial supply to both penis and
clitoris is from the internal pudendal artery, while
venous drainage is via superficial and deep dorsal
veins – I'd wager that even many urology surgeons
couldn't tell you about the nerve supply to the clitoris,
despite the fact that the equivalent male nerve maps
have been a compulsory part of their surgical syllabus
forever. Let me redress this imbalance. Nerves to the
clitoris fall into two categories. The cavernous nerves,
which supply the erectile tissue of the clitoris, are
tiny and obscure. But the ones that give this organ its
incredible sensitivity can be up to two millimetres in
diameter, and follow a clear path. Clitoral neurovas-
cular bundles, originating from the pudendal nerves,
ascend along the bony pelvis on each side before con-
vening at the corpora, whence they travel as dorsal
clitoral nerves along the top of the clitoral shaft to the
tip of its glans.

The only significant deviation in this landscape
of doubles is how the urethra forms. In the male,
a section of tissue called the urethral plate forms a
tube within the penile shaft at around eight weeks'

gestation. The remaining urogenital folds then fuse, leaving a visible line on the underside of the penis and all along the perineum, called the raphe. In females, this doesn't happen. Instead, the unfused urogenital folds become labia minora, opening into the vestibule, which encloses the vagina and urethra. But aside from this distinct fusion versus non-fusion, it is no exaggeration to say that the male and female genitalia, with penis and clitoris as key players, form in the womb as mirror images of each other.

Of course, the fact that I have a clitoris is not news to me. But until an eye-blink ago, I had no proper idea of what it was, which seems incredible given that I'm a surgeon, a mother of four, and a woman in her fifties who has been sexually active for over three decades. How would I have defined it, if pushed? As the tiny button of nerve tissue at the top end of the vulva, a sort of sensory compensation prize. I certainly had no concept of its common origins with the penis, nor that it is built and supported by all the same constituent parts, that – in an anatomical democracy – it should stand side to side with the ever-proud phallus. How on earth did I not discover this at medical school, or during the long years of my surgical training?

Curiosity on fire, I head to the hospital library. I want to go old-school, lay all the books out, inspect the diagrams, devour anatomists' different descriptions, and relish in each illustrator's personal slant. I want, for the first time, to fill in this extraordinary deficiency in my knowledge and identity. I lug the books down one by one, heavy tomes that require both arms to carry, as well as smaller books that fall across my table like a fan. There's a lot to get through but my mind feels quick and eager, and my heart skips strangely, as it often does when I'm agitated.

What I find is an information graveyard. *Last's Anatomy* (1954), one of the most respected anatomy texts available, now in its twelfth edition, makes no mention of the clitoris. The famous *Gray's Anatomy* (1858) doesn't do much better, giving the organ scant coverage, some of which is inaccurate. Even more focused texts like *Hinman's Atlas of Urologic Surgery* (1989) and Masters and Johnson's *Human Sexual Response* (1966), which you would hope would revel more in female genital anatomy, provide a disappointing lack of detail.

Has the clitoris just been discovered? Is that why it is barely mentioned by the anatomical bibles that taught me, not so long ago, all my basic anatomy? There may be a shameful dearth of information in the modern texts, but this certainly hasn't always been so. In fact, the clitoris has a rich, comprehensive, even celebratory, history. And it's one that goes back centuries.

There is competition among sixteenth-century anatomists about who first identified the clitoris. Charles Estienne mentions it in his 1545 cadaveric dissection notes, and although Italian scientist Realdo Colombo didn't officially describe the organ until four years later, he takes the biscuit for sheer excitement, eulogising the clitoris as 'the love or sweetness of Venus', likening it to the male member and immediately hitting on its importance: 'without these protuberances, women would neither experience delight in venereal embraces nor conceive any foetuses'.

Even from this early stage, the history of the clitoris looked destined to become one of alternate prominence and erasure. Aristotle is always presented as a man of great wisdom, but he thought women weren't formed properly in the womb, lacking the requisite heat to push out the more dangly genitalia men had. Those sixteenth-century giants Galen and Vesalius didn't fare much better, both drawing the false parallel between the penis and vagina that persists today, with the latter sniping that 'you can hardly ascribe this new and useless part, as if it were an organ, to healthy women'.

Despite the hum of such nonsense, the clitoris managed to stand up for itself in the seventeenth century. The outspoken midwife Jane Sharp likened it to the penis in 1671, rejoicing that it 'makes women lustful and take delight in copulation'. The wonderful anatomist Regnier de Graaf also championed it in 1672, taking his ignorant colleagues to task: 'we are extremely surprised that some anatomists make no more mention of this part than if it did not exist at all . . . in every cadaver we have so far dissected we have found it quite perceptible to sight and touch'. He also philosophically added that if women didn't have such an efficient organ of pleasure, none 'would be willing to undertake for herself such a troublesome pregnancy of nine months'. And the English surgeon William Cowper devoted a whole chapter to the clitoris in one of his textbooks.

In the eighteenth century, it was widely believed that orgasms helped women conceive. Anecdote has it that the physician to Princess Maria Theresa, asked to explain in the 1740s why she wasn't yet pregnant, responded, 'I think the vulva of Her Most Holy Majesty should be titillated before intercourse.' The following decade saw the Swiss biologist Albrecht von Haller locating female pleasure 'in the entrance of the pudendum', and explaining that the purpose of the clitoris is quite simply to 'raise the pleasure to the highest pitch'.

The nineteenth century is hard to read straight. On the one hand, female desire became increasingly pathologised. Medical textbooks warned that female lust caused problems like uterine adhesions and hypertrophy. Physician William Acton's opinion that 'a modest woman seldom desires any sexual gratification for herself' would have been typical, while Elizabeth Sheehan's 1997 account of Victorian surgeon Isaac Baker Brown's aggressive clitoridectomy surgery for women with epilepsy and psychiatric instability makes for a very chilling read.

It wasn't all bad, though. Georg Kobelt, one of the anatomists to have contributed most significantly to our understanding of the clitoris, produced a large volume of work during the 1840s, including dissections, comparative anatomy and injection studies, whose aim was to enable scrutiny of the female genitals during sexual arousal. He states, with a directness so hard to find today, 'In this essay, I have made it my principle concern to show that the female possesses a structure that in all its separate parts is entirely analogous to the male.'

Other inspiring contributions emerge from this period. British physician Henry Havelock Ellis's 1897 *Studies in the Psychology of Sex* derides the hypocrisy of denying female sexuality: 'Every woman has her own system of manifest or latent erogenic zones, and it is the lover's part in courtship to discover these zones and to develop them in order to achieve that tumescence which is naturally and properly the first stage in the sexual union.' In her 1902 *Essays in Medical Sociology*, pioneering physician Elizabeth Blackwell revels in the 'unbridled impulse of physical lust' which she argues is as natural to women as men. She refers openly to female orgasms as 'sexual spasms' and says that women crave 'the love touch' even more than coitus. And here is what Marie Stopes has to say in her 1918 text *Married Love*, words I find strangely moving: 'So widespread in Anglo-Saxon countries is the view that it is only depraved women who have such feelings, that most women would rather die than acknowledge that they *do* at times feel a physical yearning indescribable, but as profound as the hunger for food.'

The early twentieth century was also an era of mixed messages. Freud may have peddled the unhelpful view that that clitoral orgasm was a disorder found in infantile and neurotic women who had become stuck in their development and had failed to achieve the more mature and desired state of genital primacy. But many others were expressing a more emancipated view of female sexuality. The 1926 Dutch compendium *Ideal Marriage*, which ran to forty-three editions in

English, endorses extensive foreplay and cunnilingus. Home-grown British gynaecologist Helena Wright's 1930 *The Sex Factor in Marriage* exhorts women to free themselves up to pleasure and is clear in her warning that 'a wife who allows her mind to keep any unworthy ideas about sex lurking in its corners is her own worst enemy. Her body will only yield its fullest joy, will only allow her to know the experience of physical ecstasy, if her mind and soul are in active sympathy with it.' In a later publication in 1947, she goes to great pains to describe exactly what pattern of 'rhythmic friction' the clitoris responds best to, concluding that the pleasure experienced if the right technique is used is so spectacular it 'cannot be described in words'.

High-quality anatomical information was out there centuries ago. Uninhibited advice on female sexual satisfaction existed in the public domain decades before I was born. So where were these wise teachers when I was growing up? And how do we get this crucial information back into the mainstream?

The modern champion of the clitoris is an Australian urologist called Helen O'Connell. Making no bones about the fact that the clitoris expertise provided by de Graaf and Kobelt has vanished from modern sources because of 'active deletion rather than simple omission in the interests of brevity', she has written what must be the best and most detailed anatomical study of the clitoris ever published, at long last providing surgeons keen to protect the nerve function of their female as well as male urology patients a roadmap they can depend on. Someone should build a big gold statue of O'Connell. But she's certainly not on her own.

Activists like V – formerly known as Eve Ensler – continue to campaign for the rights of women and girls all over the world. Jenny Ash's wonderful TV documentary *100 Vaginas* has been broadcast by Channel 4. Artist Laura Kingsley is busy drawing clitorises on pavements and Jamie McCartney has erected a sculptural wall of multiple vulvas. In education, there are also signs of change. Canadian gynaecologist Jen Gunter has published her excellent *The Vagina Bible*. Odile Fillod's 3-D printed clitoris is now being used to teach French schoolchildren, and a broader curriculum for sex education has finally been introduced in UK schools.

I want to join this band. Even so far through my adult life, I know I feel distinctly different for learning the truth about my own sexual anatomy. Now that I realise that my reproductive organs have arisen from the same embryology as men's and that our genitals are actually very similar, now that I see the clitoris isn't just a dot on the female landscape, but rather our version of the penis, extending its fibres right through the perineum, I feel a degree more confident. Cocksure, you might say.

I'm not convinced I like the old advice for girls, to learn their own anatomy by sitting on the floor with a mirror. Today's youngsters already seem too hung up on how their vulvas look. No, I'm more for a manifesto of feeling than appearing. What I'd like to see is the next generation of young women being taught not only about the trials and tribulations of reproduction, but also their own right to sexual desire and satisfaction. Let's stop browbeating our girls with the miserable incitement to say no, and teach them instead how arousal and excitement feel, so they know when to say yes. I think we should push pleasure, for what clearer route could there be towards learning who you are? What better way to dream, and then become?

Her parents are both dead now, so there are no one's feelings left to spare. She sleeps, while the beautiful surgeon scrubs and a nurse sets two tables alongside the bed. One holds a tray full of instruments. Right-angled retractors nestle on the other's blue-draped surface. An anaesthetic assistant removes the patient's blanket and adjusts her position on the operating table by pulling her hips down to the edge of its removable section, which he then detaches. Her feet are put in stirrups, and I notice her scrotum is bald, from pre-op electrolysis.

We collect in a circle for the checklist. The theatre is wide and bright, windows looking out on the grey teeth of a London skyline and a strip of navy-green parkland below. Slim arms across her chest, Miss R states the patient's name, age and hospital number. No allergies, no metalwork, instruments all correct, any concerns? A nurse writes the operation up on the whiteboard: Vaginoplasty with Penoscrotal Inlay.

Gown- and mask-ready, headlight on, Miss R approaches, puts a drape over each leg, sticks a horizontal one over the anus, then settles on a stool. She picks up a paddle filled with chloroprep – like one of those washing-up sponges with detergent poured into its handle – and paints the perineum Tango-orange. Then she clips a fresh swab to the leg drape, asks for the diathermy to be switched on, pauses quietly for a moment, and begins.

With two tiny metal clips, she pinches the scrotum on each side, and hands them to her junior to lift high and wide, as if he were hanging a sheet on the washing line. She asks for metal ruler and pen, leaves a clear margin from the anus before starting to mark eighteen centimetres straight up along the raphe of the perineum and scrotum. She turns the line she's made into a letter T, by drawing on a horizontal cross-line of seven centimetres at the top. Joining the ends of the horizontal line to the bottom of the vertical one, she creates an outline like the shape of a kite, known as a posterior racquet handle.

With a size 10 blade, Miss R creates a skin flap, to be used in the very last stages of this operation. Stroking along the lines she has marked with a knife, she lays the blade down and picks up Gillies forceps in one hand and McIndoe scissors in the other, using them deftly to separate the skin from the underlying flesh. With her thumbs, she then locates the testes inside the denuded scrotum and works them upwards, like presents from the bottom of a Christmas stocking. She grabs each one firmly with a clip and passes them over to her assistant to hold back. The testes remind me of two encouraging thumbs-up signs in this elevated position. Tiny bleeds from perforating vessels dot through the yellow fat, and she buzzes them with the diathermy.

In the middle of the surgical field, the meaty muscle bulbospongiosus now asserts itself, smooth as a pear. She dissects down, on the hunt for the urethra and for ischiocavernosus too. The posterior scrotal arteries she needs to salvage for the new vagina run medial to this paired muscle on each side. As long as she keeps lateral, the vessels will be safe. She sighs with satisfaction as she spots them.

Her delving is deeper now, her scalpel work more effortful. It's as if she is sculpting the contour of the penis into being, and I marvel at how deeply this organ extends inside the body, how much longer it really is than what you imagine from the outside. Eventually, she reaches the central tendon of the perineum and the prostate capsule, which gleams white through all the red. The atmosphere has changed in the room. It is a crucial point in the operation, time to start making the vaginal cavity.

Feeding in a Clutton sound, a bit like a bent knitting needle, Miss R uses it to lever the penis upwards, which brings the prostate into clear view, like a bead on a string. She considers where to make her tunnel, keeping the gland at the front and the rectum behind. Inserting a Langenbeck retractor, so she can keep the white sheen of the prostate capsule in sight, she pushes into the dark now with concentration, using suction every few seconds to remove the blood that pools within her narrow surgical field. Finally, she dons the clean glove the nurse passes her, inserting her finger into the rectum and pressing forward to make sure the tunnel she's just created feels as well as looks right – prostate above, Denonvilliers' fascia below, yes, it's all good – and she makes sure she doesn't lose where she is by squeezing a swab soaked in tranexamic acid into this space, soon to become the vagina.

The vibe of the surgery lightens briefly around the more straightforward task of orchidectomy. With dartos fascia falling away like a sleeve under her slick dissection, Miss R exposes the plum of each testis. Then, she ties a thick vicryl around the base of both spermatic cords, clips and cuts off the testes, leaving the scrotum deflated. The next stage is startling though. Miss R starts degloving the penis, which involves separating the whole of its bouncy internal substance from its surrounding tubular skin with fingers and scissors. Once the inside and outside of the penis have been completely detached from each other, she shoves the inner penis back into its old home, to make it easier to do the next step.

This is to cut out exactly the right amount of glans tissue to design a perfect clitoris. She advances with care. The penile glans – with the neoclitoris marked out on it – is pulled high up in the air with a clip, still attached to the column of bulbospongiosus. It is like a surgical parody of an erection. The urethra passes through the centre of this column of penis and, from the tip of the glans, she separates it out with her knife, until it looks like a skinny grapevine, at which point she lops off its top two thirds. The short remaining length of urethra will be enough for the new female apparatus.

And now it's time for all the redundant penis to go, an astonishing thing to witness when you consider how much importance we are used to according this part of the human body. Miss R dissects out the still-valuable glans-neoclitoris, complete with nerves and vessels, before summarily tying off the corpora cavernosa, the bulky and recognisable part of the penis, cutting it free and dumping it in the dish the nurse holds. The prostate stays where it is, too tricky to dissect out.

It's time to arrange the pieces of the puzzle, a feat that wouldn't be possible if male and female genitalia weren't so fundamentally alike. With a hair-thin suture, Miss R sews the glans skin into a tiny cone which is already starting to resemble a clitoris, then fixes the end of the urethra in its new home, up against the base of the clitoris, before moving on to fashion the neo-vagina. The remaining scrotal skin and the tubular skin sheath from the penis is now divided, all the way along the raphe, before being sutured to the skin flap cut in the first stages of surgery, nearly four hours earlier. The entrance to the new vagina is crafted out of what was originally dorsal penis skin, the two free edges becoming labia minora. Carefully, she sutures the inside edge of the new labia minora to the urethral plate, which gives the peeping vagina an authentic pink, mucosal edge, that may even produce some discharge. Then, Miss R makes a clitoral foreskin by suturing skin from the top of the labia minora over what used to be the glans penis and is now the glans clitoris.

The last job is to finish the vagina. Removing the swab from the cavity, Miss R places a deep suture at the furthest end of the vaginal recess and attaches it to two points on the skin flap, which lies ready and waiting, like the flat sail of an unlaunched boat. Final sutures are placed in the skin flap, making it into a complete tubular sheath and this neo-vagina lining is finally gently pushed into its new home with a Landon retractor. The two stay sutures are tied, fixing it in place. All that remains is for Miss R to trim the scrotal skin and use its remnants to fashion the labia majora, the final frame to the genitals she has just created.

Two drains are placed for any blood that collects, and a pack is wedged into the neo-vagina, which will stay there for forty-eight hours. The nurse attaches three massive pieces of surgical tape from the patient's belly, sticking them all the way round from tummy to groin to lower back. With no testes now, she won't need

to take testosterone blockers anymore, though supple-
mental oestrogen will always be a must. She'll have to
dilate her vagina once the pack has been removed, initially three times a day, then twice, for the rest of her
life. At follow-up appointments, she will be asked key
questions to measure the success of her surgery. Can
you pee, do you have good clitoral sensation, are you
managing penetrative sex if you want it, are you happy?

The operation has taken all morning. The sun is
high now, rinsing the room with light. The surgeon
stands up from her stool and takes off her mask. She
looks at me for the first time in hours. And though I
say nothing, she knows I'm impressed. And though she
says nothing, I can see she is satisfied. And she deserves
to be. She has helped a woman become herself.

From: GWeston@hotmail.com
To: ACHDnurse@rbh.nhs.com
Subject: patient/dr with new symptoms
Date: Sunday 31 October 2023

Dear Adult Congenital Heart Disease Team,

I am a longstanding patient of Prof. A, having been diagnosed with mitral valve prolapse as a medical student more than 20 years ago. I've been under routine review since, with no worsening of my heart condition in that time.

Over the last week, I've developed recurrent and prolonged palpitations, unlike anything I've had before. I'm thinking of phoning for advice first thing tomorrow. Please let me know if I should be taking more urgent action.

Kind regards,
(Dr) Gabriel Weston (F87148)

Sent from my iPhone

Gut

Acute abdomen: sudden onset of severe abdominal pain. As on-call surgeon, you arrive to find your patient clutching their middle or too sick to move, belly rigid as a board. First, assess for signs of a life threat. Shock? You're looking at a pale, sweaty person, with low blood pressure and a racing heartbeat. Peritonitis? You'll know it straightaway because they can't move for the pain. Gangrenous bowel? The agony doesn't fit the soft clinical signs. Ruptured ectopic? The only way to exclude it is by pregnancy-testing every single woman of reproductive age. Patients like this don't have time to lose. Hook up fluids and oxygen, but don't waste another minute before calling theatre. Whatever lies inside – gunshot or stab wound, ruptured abdominal aortic aneurysm, perforated viscus, gangrenous bowel, ectopic pregnancy – only a surgeon can fix it.

For everyone else, take a breath but don't stop moving. Give pain relief while asking questions. Slide in a nasogastric tube to decompress the stomach if they're vomiting, but also inspect. Send off blood, to look for obvious things like diabetes and pancreatitis, but know that the results won't do the work for you. Then, settle the key conundrum: where is the abdominal pain coming from?

The nature of the symptoms gives clues. Colicky pain comes and goes, implying a blockage trying to free itself, like obstructed bowel or a gallstone stuck in the tight neck of the gallbladder. Dull aching discomfort with nausea is usually an inflamed viscus. Lower abdominal pain, sudden as a light-switch being flicked on, could be a twisted testis or ovary. A writhing young man has kidney stones until proven otherwise.

Mental templates also narrow the search. Embryology says the primitive foregut travels from oesophagus to the first part of the duodenum; pathology anywhere in this stretch will produce discomfort in the epigastrium, at the top of the abdomen. The midgut runs from the duodenum to the final third of the transverse colon and gives jip near the belly button. The hindgut goes from the transverse colon to the upper anal canal and generates pain above the pubic bone. It's also worth visualising the abdomen in quadrants as this calls to mind cardinal problems that arise in each: gallbladder and pancreas pain in the right upper quadrant and appendicitis in the right lower quadrant, for example.

Keep your eye on the prize but don't let it blind you. Sometimes, problems in the abdomen refer pain to other places: pancreas and spleen pathology to the left shoulder, gallbladder inflammation to the right scapula, for instance. By the same token, emergencies elsewhere – heart attack, diabetic or sickle crisis, blood clots or infections in the lungs – may declare themselves with pain in the abdomen. Still baffled? It's time to bite the bullet with a size 10 blade, slicing the patient open from xiphisternum to pubis to unveil the disaster.

It's tempting to think the Emergency Room is all drama. The truth is that doctors in this setting need to function simultaneously in two gears, alive to the fast-changing adventure of a patient's state, but with the solid knowledge base that must guide all decision-making. Here are some essential facts about the gut.

The gut snakes nine metres from mouth to anus, and is divided into functional sections. The first of these is the oesophagus. Twenty-five centimetres long and two centimetres wide, this fibromuscular tube propels what we eat to the stomach. Swallowing takes twenty different pairs of muscles and we do it more than 2,000 times a day, mainly without thinking.

The stomach is a temporary bank for storing and breaking down food. When empty, it contracts into deep folds called rugae, which smooth out as it fills. As soon as a bolus arrives from the oesophagus, the stomach begins churning, a vigorous up-and-down movement quite different to the coordinated peristaltic waves that travel in a straight direction from the top to the bottom of the gut. In the space of two hours, big bites are mashed into tiny pieces and parsed through the pyloric sphincter as a soupy mixture called chyme.

Looping six metres from the pylorus of the stomach to the ileocaecal valve, the small bowel is the mecca for digestion and absorption. Subdivided into three further sections – the duodenum, jejunum and ileum – the whole of its internal surface is plush as a shag-pile carpet, tiny projections called villi expanding the available surface area through which nutrient molecules can pass and enter the circulation.

The final part of the gut is the large bowel, a cartoon-fat sweep which starts at the ileocaecal valve and ends five feet later at the rectum. Arranged like a portico within which the small intestine runs amok, its main job is to extract water and form solid faeces.

Any rookie wanting to perform their first solo appendicectomy must be able to distinguish small from large bowel, since the appendix is situated at the junction of the two. Make a Pfannenstiel incision in the right iliac fossa. Part muscle layers and cut a hole in the peritoneum. Stick a finger in and hook up a bit of gut. It's not enough to rely on the calibre of the large intestine being wider. Key are the taenia coli, three stripes of muscle which run lengthwise along the colon's outer surface. If you feed loops of intestine through your fingers until the point where they appear, you will find yourself at the caecum, from which the appendix dangles.

We surgeons sometimes act like we own anatomy. And perhaps it's no wonder. Since our ancestors first peeped through gladiatorial flesh wounds, most of the naming of parts has been achieved by subsequent generations painstakingly adding to and amending each other's operative findings. But here's a caveat. If you hand descriptive rights on the human body over to surgeons, what you'll get is a surgical view. This isn't the same as the truth. We rush our patients to theatre and stand making pronouncements about the visceral landscape only we have the privilege of looking at, without stopping to think what might be cast in the shadow of our gaze. We zoom in on those parts that offer us a heroic role to play, barely acknowledging that other emergencies may be unfolding outside our frame of reference. So, when a mysterious gut disease we don't know how to fix starts wreaking havoc on our wards, it's hard to know what shocks us more: our impotence, or that our long-held assumptions about what this organ is for, and how it works, are about to change forever.

Clostridioides difficile is the leading cause of hospital-acquired diarrhoea worldwide. Lucky patients might get away with a few days of diarrhoea, nausea, abdominal cramping and fever, but – in extreme cases – infection with this bug causes a widespread inflammatory condition called pseudomembranous colitis which can result in bowel perforation, sepsis and death. Accorded the highest level of threat by the Centers for Disease Control and Prevention, *C. diff* is a massive problem, infecting half a million and killing 30,000 in the US alone every year. And although it used to be confined to frail old people in hospital, the condition is now cropping up in the community among children, pregnant women, and other healthy adults.

Unseemly though it is, I can't help taking a thrill in the sheer resourcefulness of the bug that does all the damage. Rampant in soil, water and the intestinal tract, *C. diff* has two different guises: a spore for transmission and a vegetative form for destruction. Spores are the most resilient cellular form on the planet and can survive in a dormant state for decades. This one is built like a gobstopper, its arsenal encased in seven different protective shells, inuring it to oxygen, extremes of temperature, alcohol, disinfectants and radiation. The outermost layer even has little projections to help it stick to hospital bedding.

Once swallowed, the dormant spore passes, unperturbed by the acid onslaught of the stomach, into the small intestine. In a healthy gut nothing happens. But, if its usual chemical environment is disrupted, the spore is able to germinate. Roused to its vegetative state, C. diff does two things. First, it configures itself into a mother cell and a forespore. The forespore is the baby and once it achieves what is known poetically as phase-bright status, it splits off to form a new dormant bug. The remaining vegetative bacterium is now free to unleash itself, discharging powerful toxins which penetrate the target cells of the large intestine, and turn our guts to pulp.

When I was at medical school, we students loved to characterise bacteria as villains, the better to revel in how to thrash them with antibiotics. C. diff fits this bill perfectly, both in its flamboyant pathogenicity and its susceptibility to the powerful antimicrobial agent vancomycin. Lately, though, this microbe has become a virtuoso at adapting itself. Outbreaks in Europe and North Asia in the 2000s were the result of a new hypervirulent strain which produces a binary toxin. In 2005, 316 different forms of the bug were isolated in Europe, 82 of them drug-resistant. Ribotype 078, previously found only in pigs and domestic animals, is now the main cause of human infections in the Netherlands and has spread to the UK. As our pharmacological prowess has waned, we've had to confront a paradox, which is that while some individuals suffer debilitating symptoms or even die as a result of infection with this bacterium, one in ten of us are able to host it in our gut with absolutely no ill effects. Focusing our attention on the marauding microbe has distracted us from seeing that what really determines a patient's outcome is the background environment of their gut. The precise chemical milieu that renders some patients vulnerable is almost always the result of having been treated for another infection with antibiotics. Yes, it's that crazy. The gold-standard therapy for *C. diff* is the selfsame class of drugs that causes the condition in the first place.

Now, it's certainly true some of this wisdom is new. Compared to the old lab technique of isolation and culture – prodigiously difficult to pull off with gut bacteria, since few of them survive long enough outside their anaerobic environment to be studied like this – powerful modern informatics have revealed a hidden universe of hundreds of trillions of viruses, fungi, yeasts and bacteria which make our bodies their home, ninety-nine per cent of which reside in the gut. Research has also showed us what they do. Bacteria extract nutritional goodies, especially in times of food scarcity. They break down fibre into short-chain fatty acids, which regulate sugar metabolism and appetite. They make vitamins by a process of fermentation. But they operate well beyond the gut's traditional remit of digestion and absorption. Gut bacteria actually keep us healthy. In the case of C. *diff*, simply having a gut with a rich array of different species keeps the microbe in balance with its neighbours, and stops it taking over and causing disease.

You'd think these headlines about the importance of gut diversity must be hot off the press. How else to explain the fact that antibiotics are still the first-line treatment for C. *diff* in hospitals across this country? But it isn't so. As far back as 1886, Austrian paediatrician Theodor Escherich described the rich variety of infant gut bacteria, including their role in the decomposition of food. Just before the turn of the twentieth century, Henry Tissier successfully treated a group of children suffering from gastrointestinal disease with a concoction of bacteria taken from healthy breastfeeding babies. During the First World War, microbiologist

Alfred Nissle developed and patented gelatine capsules which contained a particular strain of E. coli as a treatment for dysentery in soldiers.

It's not as if we've been living in complete ignorance about *C. diff* either. First isolated in 1893 by an American surgeon called John Finney, a few decades later it was declared to be a completely normal part of the infant gut flora by Ivan Hall and Elizabeth O'Toole. In the mid-1970s, John Bartlett published a study which demonstrated antibiotics could provoke *C. diff* in hamsters and, by the end of the decade, two further papers had proved a causal link between antibiotics and *C. diff*-associated pseudomembranous colitis in humans.

Nosocomial is the term for an illness a patient contracts while in hospital. Iatrogenic describes a disease that's unwittingly caused by the interference of a doctor. We assume these events are unavoidable. So why are thousands of our patients still dying annually of a condition we're responsible for, but aren't treating wisely, despite all the available evidence? It turns out I'm not the only one who's baffled.

Providence, Rhode Island. In a fresh, sunny operating theatre, decked in pink scrubs like those the gynae doctors in *Grey's Anatomy* wear, I am waiting to meet Dr K, one of the modern pioneers of a very different treatment for *C. diff*. A laminated factsheet, printed in primary colours and stuck to the wall, tells me the basics. Faecal microbiota transplant (FMT) is indicated for those patients whose *C. diff* infections are either recurring or not responsive to standard treatment. The procedure involves transferring bacteria from healthy donor stool into a sick recipient's intestine, the aim being to restore a diverse range of bacteria in their gut.

The double doors open and Dr K walks in, all smiles and glossy American hair, chatting to an elderly woman being wheeled by a couple of nurses. Once the hospital bed is fixed in position, we introduce ourselves and, as Dr K checks her equipment, she tells me how she got started.

A few years back, a young woman turned up at her clinic with an all-too-common history of months of suffering from diarrhoea after taking antibiotics for a quite separate infection. But this was no usual patient. With a stack of evidence from the internet and a boyfriend in tow happy to be her donor, she cut straight to the chase. She wanted to be given a stool transplant. Initially taken aback – Dr K wasn't used to patients telling her what to do – this doctor performed the radical clinical courtesy of keeping an open mind, and promised to read the notes her patient had put together.

In a nutshell, this is what she learned. In the fourth

century, a Chinese Daoist called Ge Hong administered faecal suspensions orally to patients who had diarrhoea from food poisoning. Ancient Bedouins routinely ate camel faeces for dysentery, a habit revived by German soldiers in Africa during the Second World War. In 1958, a surgeon called Ben Eiseman published an account of successfully treating pseudomembranous colitis with faeces. And a gastroenterologist called Thomas Borody was currently using healthy donor stool to treat refractory cases of *C. diff* in Australia, with great outcomes.

Dr K was bowled over. Despite cynicism from most of her colleagues, she went ahead and performed her first faecal transplant in 2008. And when the young woman's symptoms disappeared completely after a single treatment, she decided to set up an FMT service, making the therapy available to others and gathering data on all her results. In 2013, she found herself in good company when a landmark randomised controlled trial in the *New England Journal of Medicine* declared FMT so much more effective than antibiotics at treating *C. diff* that researchers had to halt the study early, as it felt unethical to withhold the new treatment from the control group. Multiple subsequent studies have shown FMT to be more than ninety per cent effective, making it one of the most successful cures in medical history.

It's slick too. With her patient curled up on one side, Dr K introduces the narrow scope, and pink colonic mucosa blooms into view on the screen in front of us. A nurse dressed in lemon yellow holds out a plastic jug, in which five 60 ml syringes stand, pretty as stems in a vase, full of strained and saline-diluted donor stool. As she empties the unlikely elixir into her patient's sigmoid colon, she tells me how sceptical colleagues who once laughed her off now queue up for training. The whole procedure is done within ten minutes and, when I accompany Dr K the following morning to check on the patient's response, we find the previously frail lady euphoric. After just one treatment, her chronic diarrhoea has completely resolved.

Later that day, I hop on a train to Boston to visit Openbiome, the not-for-profit stool bank where Dr K gets all her samples, set up in 2012 by a couple of MIT graduate students, after one of their friends recovered from chronic *C. diff* thanks to a DIY faecal transplant. There's a lot to marvel at – the energy of the CEO who welcomes me in, smooth-chinned as a schoolboy, the giant fridges, in which thousands of square frosted bottles of donor faeces are shelved in neat rows, the sheer rate of expansion of this start-up which, having initially occupied no more than a small corner of an MIT lab, has since become a full-scale operation delivering 70,000 pre-screened, ready-to-use samples to a thousand clinical destinations. Perhaps what strikes me most, though, is the same curiously anecdotal nature to Openbiome's origins that I also noticed in Dr K's story.

Medicine can be a conformist profession. The barnyard whiff of faecal transplant and a fear of ridicule have stood in the way of progress for generations. In the end, it has taken a group of patients to look out for their own interests and persuade a few brave medics and entrepreneurs to take a punt with them. Prepared to see potential where others were too prissy to look, this tenacious lot have now armed themselves with evidence and are pushing a remarkable medical treatment right into the mainstream.

As a junior doctor, I often got doused in my patients' vomit and shit. I didn't mind though. The trick was to look on the clinical bright side. A teenager barfing up paracetamol would escape a liver transplant. The colour and smell of an old man's faeces might signal occult blood and help save his life. The contents of normal guts, however, were of less interest. I had been taught that the sole purpose of the alimentary canal was to extract nutrients from food. The further along this tube you went, the less interesting its cargo became and, by the time you reached the colon, all that was left were fibrous remnants and a bunch of bugs, a stinking concoction fit for nothing but the U-bend.

All that has changed. Extending well beyond the immediate emergency of *C. diff* and hospital-acquired diarrhoea, we're learning more every day about the importance of these previously disregarded life forms, why it matters to have a diverse gut flora, and the numerous pathological consequences that may occur if this balance gets disrupted.

It turns out microbes don't just exert effects on each other locally. One of the biggest revelations in recent gut science has been that this organ isn't a simple tube after all, but the largest sensory organ we have, the most receptive interface that exists between a person and the outside world. With more immune cells than across the rest of the body put together, and an internal surface area a hundred times bigger than the skin, the gut is held within an elaborate harness we now call the gut-brain, which contains up to 600 million neurons. This plexus of nerves doesn't just chivvy food along. It is like a delicate switchboard, continually integrating information about what we've eaten, our blood chemistry, our immune state and our microbiology, data then conveyed straight to the brain along a large nerve called the vagus.

In 2004, a landmark study by the Japanese

gastroenterologist Gota Sudo showed that mice raised with no gut flora have a disrupted stress response, which can be partly corrected by colonising their intestines with normal bacteria. Since then, countless experiments have demonstrated that the brain, the gut and its resident bacteria coexist in an intimate three-way circuit. Changes in any of these three sites affect the others. Alterations in gut bacteria impact on aspects of intestinal function such as secretion, speed of digestion and gut-wall permeability, but they can also influence our mental state. In turn, how we feel can influence how the gut behaves, as well as the composition of its microbiota. Nine tenths of the research ever published on the gut has blossomed in the past twenty years and is revolutionising the way we think, not only about normal physiology, but diseases such as anxiety and depression, schizophrenia, autism, multiple sclerosis and irritable bowel syndrome.

Yes – extrapolating from animal models should be done with caution. Sure – where the gut-brain axis is concerned – there's a long way to go before we can confidently make the leap from correlation to causation. But I, for one, need no more persuading.

At the start of university, I move into a flat with three other students. The guy who owns the place is a Scot who doesn't believe in central heating. There are other ways to keep warm, he says, like eating meat to raise the core temperature, or growing a beard. Sometimes he goes to the local butcher and brings home rabbit skins which he soaks in the bath before sewing them into furry jerkins and boots to wear around the flat with his kilt. My second flatmate is tidy, with a racing bike and a daily paper, and studies English literature like me. The last is a floppy ex-Etonian who stays in bed all day, smoking and listening to reggae.

Who says student life has to be wild? My room in this top-floor flat is huge and has a hot-air-balloon-high view out over the Edinburgh sky, with its wide pinks and purples, the rooftops like matchboxes far below. I wake each morning to my Swan Teasmade, the click of its light and the friendly growl of water bubbling from tank to pot. I pedal hard out of Stock-bridge and up the steep curve of the Mound and, in the afternoons, I fly downhill with no brakes on, the Firth of Forth in the distance, cheek-chilled. I chat with my bookish flatmate in the kitchen over cheese toasties. On the weekends, I walk up Arthur's Seat with friends and swim at the Glenogle Baths and go to the pub. I write essays at my desk with woollen gloves on, woozy from the Calor Gas heater. And as nights draw in, I feel the comfort of the boys nearby, while my window rattles and ice-patterns form on the inside of the glass.

In my final year, I start dating one of my lecturers. He teaches Scottish literature and is known for not having sex with Southerners. I joke he can't resist the fact I'm the only student ever to have read the whole of Hugh MacDiarmid's *A Drunk Man Looks at the Thistle*. I figure I'm going up in the world, exchanging the last vestiges of childhood for something more sophisticated, life with a real grown-up who has formed tastes and politics, and a marriage behind him. When he asks me, I don't think twice about moving in, packing up the room in which I have been so happy, swapping the easy disregard of my flatmates for a house that has central heating and a fridge with fancy food in it, and a bookshelf neatly arranged with revolutionary literature. I have no idea that what I am doing is giving up my freedom.

I never stop to consider I am making a mistake. Even as the weeks pass and the initial shine wears off and the light cools and darkens. Even as the months go by and I experience a painful nostalgia when I cycle past my old flat. Even as the seasons change and I tell myself it's natural to be less excited about getting home in the evening, too callow to know that passion should cool to companionship not constraint, that the questioning which awaits me each evening when I return from lectures or the library – where have I been, who with, what kind of friendship is it, how do they look at me, do I like it? – is far from benign.

I don't exactly have regrets. The change that happens is more in my body than my mind, call it a gut feeling. I get stomach aches and soon they're bad enough to keep me home. I am often nauseated and this makes me nervous about going to lectures, so I fall behind. And before I know it, my confidence has gone and even going outside becomes daunting.

Through the GP's window, I hear noises of gravel and birds. These small sounds seem big because we are sitting in silence. Compared to home, with its rapid fire of questions, it's peaceful here, a place my thoughts can expand and roam. What would it be like to be a doctor, I wonder? On the far side of the room is the neat blue-papered couch where he examined me the first time, and glass-fronted cabinet with thick, purposeful books. On the wall behind him are three tatty posters with the same human outline, but different internal structures defined – bones, blood vessels and lymphatics. His desk is always a tower of paperwork, patient files mixed with journals and letters. Various medical instruments lie in a heap by his computer. Today, an old-style doctor's bag, leathery and humbug-shaped, hangs open at his feet, stuff tipping out.

He plays with the rubber ends of the stethoscope round his neck and straightens his tie, smiles. I look at his desk, his instruments for peering in eyes and ears, and for listening. I remember my previous Edinburgh flat, my own lovely clutter of pictures and pens, books and papers. At some point he asks after my symptoms, whether the antispasmodics – the only available treatment for irritable bowel syndrome – are helping at all. But only a few of his questions focus on my medical complaint. He favours another tack which baffles me at the time, though it makes complete sense to me now. Do I have any new worries? Am I sleeping? How often do I laugh and take the fresh air? He asks after my happiness.

Within days of finishing my degree, not even waiting for graduation, I pack up all my belongings. The carriage I board on the train heading south from Waverley station has a group of women on it, already pissed as newts having begun their carousing as they pulled out of Inverness. I get on with boxes full of my stuff and a tear-stained face and they just enfold me. And soon my face is dry again and I am drinking whisky and telling them all about the last four years of my life which, until that moment, felt like they were everything but, with the moving of the train and the telling of my story, now start to unhook, their grip loosening, seams unravelling, so that I feel the special texture of things that are over, and realise for the first time that the past isn't simply passive but actual, a bolt of experience that you can choose to put behind you, drawing out only those threads that glitter. And when I remember this journey, though I know it happened on a train, what I see in my mind's eye is something else. I am with the Scottish women on the back deck of a ferry, and there is the roar of the engine, and salt-petrol in my nostrils and, down below, the churning froth of the wake coming out of the stern of the boat. And though the bulk of the ferry prevents me from seeing what lies ahead, there is no doubting the dwindling of the shore behind, a life already refused, that I am tilting further and further away from with every real, up-close instant of the here and now.

E. M. Forster's *Howards End* begins with the epigraph 'Only connect'. As a teenager sitting in an English lesson, I remember being baffled. But now, in medicine, as in the rest of life, these words mean the world. A tiny but dangerous organism like *C. diff* can't be understood in isolation from its neighbouring community of microbes. The vital organs we once saw as separate are in constant communication. The story of faecal microbiota transplant illustrates to an occasionally defensive medical fraternity that we should welcome rather than disregard the rich testimony of our patients. Science is nothing without seeing. We don't always know where the next revelation is coming from. And sometimes, the truth may be felt in the body long before we're able to grasp it with the mind.

Womb

I am sitting in front of a womb in a jar. This one is a beauty, its parts still plump despite years stewing in formalin. An old textbook, fat as a folder of wallpaper swatches, lies next to me. I turn the jar this way and that, to try and get the best view. I compare what's in front of me with facts from the book. The uterus consists of three parts: the fundus at the top, the body in the middle and the cervix below. It is eight centimetres long, five centimetres across and four centimetres thick, and sits between bladder and rectum. Pins stick out from structures in the jar and correspond to tiny labels on its wooden base, reassuring me of features even a child could pick out – the ovaries and fallopian tubes, as well as the less familiar broad and round ligaments. I read the age-old comment that the uterus is shaped like a pear.

Before long, my head sinks down on the book, which smells just like my grandpa used to. Of course the old-fashioned way of studying anatomy isn't doing it for me. No wonder I feel uninspired by a gallery of dead specimens, arranged like Snow Whites in their glass cases, and by the pages of anatomy hillocking beside me. I've had far more exciting views of the uterus than this.

Years ago, when I was working as a medical TV presenter for the BBC, I was asked to make a trip to Gothenburg in Sweden, to film one of the world's first womb transplants. The surgeon, Prof. B, having spent his career researching the idea and trying it out on primates, had finally been given ethics approval and enough funding to perform a small number of these operations on women. The transplant we were invited to was only the second he had done and would be attended by a large number of international gynaecologists and vascular surgeons, as well as our camera crew.

Surrogacy is illegal in Sweden, and Prof. B explained to me that womb transplant might therefore offer women born without a womb, or those requiring hysterectomy because of cancer, their only chance to have their own biological child. He added that there are currently 15,000 women of reproductive age in this position in the UK alone. I was interviewing him on camera and trying to keep my face neutral, so as not to have to retake the shot. But inside, my thoughts were all over the place. Is this surgery the way forward?

Shouldn't adoption be encouraged when people can't have their own child? Wouldn't it be better to use whatever funds are available to subsidise a few rounds of IVF for infertile couples, rather than underwriting exorbitant and experimental operations?

But a keen appetite for surgery often trumps finer objections. I soon became distracted by watching adjoining operating theatres being prepared for the day's patients, a mother and daughter, one intent on doing anything to help the other have a baby. And instead of the technical aspects of the operation ahead that would usually preoccupy me, I found myself musing on the strangeness of this precise Swedish womb, lying in the soft interior of its lifelong home, soon to make the journey into a body it previously gave birth to. A womb which once encapsulated a baby girl was about to be encased within the adult she had become, to bring forth the next generation of child, and its original owner's grandchild. Any organ transplant has a mind-bending quality, but this one seemed amazing on a whole new level.

I've never seen the inside of a woman's body receive so much attention as on that day – clever, burly shoulders from Europe and America forming a ledge over which I craned to see what was happening. The need to preserve blood vessels in an optimum state for replumbing made this hysterectomy go on for hours longer than usual. At last, as the sky changed from daylight to the deep blue which had greeted us when we entered the hospital early that morning, I stood back and watched the professor lifting to the light the newborn uterus, everyone else's arms rising up in unison, a chorus of applause and wonder echoing around the gleaming room. I saw this in front of me and I also watched it being filmed, the black cube of the camera monitor giving me a sense of how this present reality might seem later on, edited and preserved for a television audience's delight. Little did I know, as I took my choreographed position a few paces behind the surgeon, to be filmed following him while he carried the precious organ down the corridor in a silver dish to its new home, that another drama was beginning to unfold deep inside my own womb.

Learning which arteries provide oxygen to every part of the body is an essential building block of surgical training. Blood supply to the stomach, complicated as hell and yet beautifully intuitive. Blood supply to the brain, known enchantingly as the Circle of Willis. Blood supply to the lower limb, the thorax, the hand the foot and, yes, even the uterus. I've memorised all these details so many times that I will probably be muttering them, along with random obscenities and Latin declensions, when I'm old and dementing. But I was never taught about the part I now find most fascinating – the network of tiny intricate vessels that enable menstruation.

Imagine you are inside a womb. The tissue you are pressed up against is called the endometrium and is composed of functional and basal layers. It sits on top of the muscular myometrium. Put aside any squeamishness you might feel and appreciate that, for renewal on a grand scale, the body doesn't have a single other show like menstruation. Every month, for forty years or so, the uterus primes itself for the possibility of conception. If this were Christmas, the womb wouldn't just buy a bit of crappy tinsel. It would go all out, lugging in a tree, sending cards, peeling spuds and sprouts, stirring the cake and hanging out the stockings. For every month of a woman's reproductive life, the uterus has to be ready, so that if a tiny fertilised embryo should land there, it will find all the conditions it needs to embed and grow. But for the thousands of times this event doesn't take place, the womb also needs to be able to cancel its revels, tidy up and go in a flash. Its unique blood supply is what allows this to happen.

Arising from the main uterine arteries are two types of smaller ones. Straight arteries poke through the myometrium into the basal layer of the endometrium and are short and permanent. But it's the spiral arteries which wow me. These penetrate both layers of endometrium. If a pregnancy takes place, they develop into capacious vessels which supply the placenta and help nourish the growing foetus. But in the commoner situation of menstruation, they behave differently. Growing slightly faster than the surrounding functional endometrium, they coil themselves up, to keep in line with it. They are like daisies, pushing through a growing lawn, if those daisies were mindful to keep their little faces at exactly the same height as the grass around them.

At the end of a menstrual cycle, if there is no fertilised egg, ovarian hormone levels drop. This causes the functional layer to shrink a bit, which means that the spiral arteries, those perky daisies sitting in now tatty grass, have to coil up even more to stay in line. Being so tightly coiled restricts blood flow through these arteries, making the functional layer shrink even more. The gradual withering of the surface layer causes toxic substances to be released. And then tissue death gathers pace, until the whole network of little vessels ruptures. The myometrial layer of the uterus responds by contracting, and the resulting pain and bleeding is what we women experience as a period.

What's the most important organ? People revel in the chicken-and-egg conundrum, the battle between heart and brain. The heart must be in charge, some argue, because it supplies blood, and therefore life, to everything else. The brain is king because, without its instructions, the heart wouldn't know how to beat. But how about which organ is the coolest?

I feel for the hard ridge of my pelvic scar. For the job it does in pregnancy and childbirth, you couldn't find a more impressive organ than the uterus. I'm still gobsmacked by the feats my own womb has performed, two children born vaginally and two by caesarean section. I'm also drawn to the organ's reproductive biology. For starters, there's the question of how it goes from being tiny to huge to tiny again, over a mere few months. But even more intriguing is the fact that, in order for a pregnancy to succeed, the womb must employ contradictory powers. It has to remain quiescent until labour and then become extremely dynamic. How does this work?

Partly, the womb's versatility is a matter of structure. The myometrium – the muscular wall of the uterus – is made of bundles of smooth muscle cells. Prompted by the foetus, the pregnant woman's body produces extra oestrogen and progesterone, and these hormones cause an increase in both the number and the size of these cells in the womb wall. Muscle fibres that were previously just 50 micrometres in length spring to 600 micrometres in the pregnant uterus, and they course in different directions, bolstering the tissue's overall tensile strength. Imagine a woman with her lover standing behind her embracing her pregnant abdomen. The lover's hands change position, encircle her this way and that, miming the orientation of the circular and longitudinal muscle fibres lying below.

Even during the early stages of pregnancy, when it is essential the uterus remains calm so as to retain the growing foetus, the myometrium primes itself by trying out small and regular contractions. These are detectable as early as seven weeks' gestation and increase in both intensity and frequency as the pregnancy blooms. The womb is flexing its powers early on, but holding back enough to ensure it preserves its precious contents. The success of this depends on a strong fibrous cervix, the door that must remain shut, and also on increasing levels of progesterone. As the uterus continues to grow, this hormone acts to limit muscle activity to a very localised patch.

A healthy pregnancy arriving at term turns things around. A variety of changes, partly maternal and partly foetal, heralds the start of labour. The cervix thins out and a series of contractions along the length of the uterus results in birth. Strong, productive uterine activity depends on electrical events called action potentials within each smooth muscle cell, which ensure contractions are multiple, coordinated and connected. Gap junctions are channels of low electrical resistance made of protein which increase in number at the end of a pregnancy, encouraging the spread of contractions throughout the entire womb.

Although pacemaker cells in the heart have been known about for decades, the question of exactly which cells in the womb initiate the cascade of contractions which result in birth is still hotly debated. Some believe they must be located in the womb's fundus, it's just that we haven't identified them yet. Others speculate that the starter-gun for electrochemical activity in the uterus can originate in any single myometrial smooth muscle cell. Something called a membrane oscillator has even been postulated, a kind of spontaneous moving and shaking of the perimeter of the cell which gets it electrochemically excited and sets everything else off.

There's so much to marvel at in the anatomy and physiology of this organ, but the womb certainly isn't a problem-free zone, as just a few stats from the WHO and Action Aid show. 295,000 women die each year in pregnancy and childbirth. Ninety-four per cent of those deaths occur in low-income countries and are medically preventable. The risk of perinatal mortality is especially high for girls under fifteen, in whom childbirth is the second-highest cause of death worldwide. Forty-one per cent of women do not have access to abortion and 23,000 women a year die from unsafely attempting to terminate their pregnancies. In view of recent retrograde legislation in the US, this situation seems likely to get worse.

Obstetric stats clearly show that women are at highest risk from their wombs during pregnancy and procreation, but cultural history would have us believe it's the fallow uterus that causes the most havoc. It's hard not to read a deep anxiety about female anatomy into the prehistoric notion that women might possess up to seven copies of this organ. And the ancient Greeks' and Egyptians' belief that the uterus roamed around the body causing harm to whichever organ it paused near seems equally twitchy. But the Victorians take the biscuit. Their catch-all diagnosis of hysteria was used to explain disorders as diverse as epilepsy, PTSD and depression, as well as to pathologise female unruliness. Known victims include the authors Edith Wharton, Virginia Woolf and Charlotte Perkins Gilman. Suffragettes were treated as hysterics in prison. Meanwhile American physician S. Weir

Mitchell achieved star status for his 'rest cure', a regime which imposed long spells in bed and complete intellectual privation on supposedly afflicted females. At least back then, the message seemed to be that the only safe womb was a married and pregnant one.

We may be tempted to laugh this off as quaint, but the womb still holds women in a special social, political and personal thrall. It's not just that misogynist myths are slow to debunk – the diagnosis of hysteria wasn't removed from the *Diagnostic and Statistical Manual of Mental Disorders* until 1980, and it only became illegal for a man to demand intercourse from his wife in 1991. There are new problems too. Better obstetric imaging brings medical benefits, but also accentuates a tension which has always existed between the rights of the mother and her unborn foetus, known in sociological circles as the 'maternal–foetal conflict'. And while the epigenetic revelation that a person's physical, psychological and social well-being can be partly traced to their time in the womb may help women make healthy decisions during pregnancy, the paternalistic dangers of such research are not trivial. It's still possible for a pregnant woman to order a drink in the UK without attracting stares, but there are many parts of the world where this would be unthinkable. In the US, plenty of women have been prosecuted since the turn of the century, some for murder, for 'chemically endangering' their foetuses by consuming drugs or alcohol while pregnant.

In 2017, a team of scientists at the Children's Hospital of Philadelphia kept a pre-viable lamb foetus alive for four weeks in an amniotic fluid-filled bio-bag, attached by its umbilical cord to a mechanical placenta, and it appeared to grow quite normally. I've witnessed a womb transplant with my own eyes. Technologically speaking, it feels like the sky's the limit. But, in terms of our preconceptions, how far have we really come? Don't we still live in a society which values women primarily as gestators, with a punitively narrow view of how that role should be experienced? Where women who struggle to conceive feel ashamed, where those who elect not to have children are treated with suspicion? Where getting pregnant by accident and having an abortion continues to carry a huge stigma? Where – if writer Rachel Cusk's piercingly honest book *A Life's Work* is anything to go by – expressing even the slightest degree of ambivalence about the mixed blessing of pregnancy, childbirth and motherhood is enough to get one burnt at the proverbial stake?

Well, all I can say is this. If we women are to be held to account for our wombs, since the way we live with our uteruses and the decisions we make about them end up being so damn personal, then the only way to talk honestly about this marvellous organ is to get personal right back.

Gothenburg. Across the room from me, the director is up on her stool, balancing the weight of the camera on her shoulder and pointing the lens down into the patient's open pelvis to get what she's been waiting for all day, the money shot. No eyes on me, I sink into a chair. It won't be much longer, surely? Hysterectomies are usually swift. I'm not sure why I'm so tired, though there is a reason. Deep inside my body, unusual new life is forming. A fertilised egg has recently achieved zygote status. Perhaps this is the exact point where the blastocyst splits, creating not one but two potential lives. I sit on the theatre stool, looking out of the window, quite unaware of these internal events that are going to change my life forever.

A few weeks on, I go for a scan. The blue paper which I usually place under other people's bums is now under me. I see my bare knees and feel the coolness of the smeary jelly and, before I know it, the sonographer is telling me the joyous news. Just imagine, she says, you are pregnant with identical twins. She can see this quite clearly, as they share a sac. Look at them, she points, what a blessing. The screen is black and swimmy, the room is brown with the dim glow of an anglepoise lamp.

Sometime later, I am at home alone. I have recovered from the shock and I am done with making my friends laugh with my news. I think of how the womb is a crazy thing. I have seen it raised into the sky like a butterfly in an operating theatre, I have watched a roomful of men pore over its blood supply and tend to its tiny vessels. I have witnessed a mother laid out on a slab to allow the evisceration of her womb. And I have followed a man down a corridor, paces behind him as he hurried that womb in his hands, in a shiny metal dish, vessels winged out to the sides ready to be laid so gently into a cut-open daughter. Here it is, my love, my present to you. Here is the house that Jack built, lay your own little eggs in it.

But all that is not as wonderful or strange as this. I look from the kitchen window into the garden. I feel stretched with the conflict between gratitude and not-readiness for what is happening to me. I have twice experienced the tight mesh of love and imprisonment which is motherhood and I'm not sure how I'll manage the doubling of this load. I have been told about the risks of my pregnancy now that I'm in my forties, and they are considerable. I am old, these tiny foetuses, not yet bigger than my little finger, are to share a blood supply and they might not manage to do that. They might not do well. They might both die or they might live but not be healthy. I would like my brain to reassert itself and my brain did not plan this.

The months go by, and soon it is the end of my pregnancy and someone is coming to fetch me from the ward. I am wearing a gown and trainers. I still have my pants on because there's a slit down the back and it's a bit of a trek from this part of the hospital to the operating theatre. I am walking there but I won't be walking back. Down in the foyer, people do the things I have done, and will do again. Someone pauses close to the big picture of the elephant and puts their face right up against it: is it a photo? No, it's a beautiful pains-taking work in pencil. A woman with a new pregnancy holds her tummy dramatically as she goes towards the clinic. There is the fish tank and the card shop. Here is the whole story of the last thirty-six weeks, complete with anxious appointments and scans, here is the cup of tea bought from that café, there is the growing excitement spangled in the colourful mobile which hangs through all the glassy floors. Here are the other people coming to visit and to die. I am on the brink of something important and the moment brims beyond anything I can capture.

I sit sideways on the bed and bend as far forwards as

two big, about-to-be-born babies will allow me to. The anaesthetist guddles around in my back to site the spinal anaesthetic. I notice two cots in the corner and can't believe they have anything to do with me. The space between this now and that then seems galaxy-wide. The anaesthetist tips me back and sprays the length of my naked body with something I don't feel until its freezing wetness on my neck suggests to him the spinal has done its work. Raise your left leg, raise your right, he says and when I can't he knows I'm ready. The lovely obstetrician comes and talks to me, reassuring me that I still exist, am actually a part of what is happening in this room. I try to comfort myself with the thought that I am usually in her position, and will be again.

My mouth does a good enough job of talking back. I can hear the words out there, like a beacon against this absolute interiority, and I feel the acutest sense of living, which must be a bit what it's like to be just about to die. Within my skin are three beating hearts. We are all lying back on the operating table. I am the shell, within which is the other big shell, my womb, which is nearly as big as me. I am meant to be standing up with the knife in my hand, that's how I like it. But I am lying down, full of heart and womb and my twin girls' hearts and wombs. She cuts me open.

*

In Virginia Woolf's *To the Lighthouse*, Lily Briscoe stands at her canvas on a clifftop and looks down on Mr Ramsay and his two children in a boat. And then we are in that boat, and they are looking back at Lily Briscoe.

Some women swerve childbirth altogether, daring to claim what men have, the rich and adventurous lives they correctly calculate will be almost impossible to combine with motherhood in today's world. Others set out their stall in the act of procreation, defying the patriarchal medicalisation of birth by having their babies at home, assisted by trusted midwives or doulas, in the company of family. Some video the event, so that they can watch it back on repeat and process the astonishing physical facts of bearing a child in the cold light of day. Some integrate the mystery of childbirth literally, by eating their placenta or planting it under a tree in the garden.

For others, recovering from the sucker punch of childbirth and early motherhood is more humdrum. It is simply a matter of getting back up on one's feet. A few months after my twins are born, I email the obstetric surgeon who delivered them, and ask if I might come and watch her perform the same operation I had. I want to watch her go through exactly the same surgical steps on someone else, I explain, because that's the only way I'll ever really be able to understand what happened to my body that day.

And so it is that I find myself standing, fully scrubbed, in the same theatre where I was so recently a patient, while a young woman thirty-six weeks pregnant with identical twin girls walks in with her husband, backlit by the beams of a pale winter sun. Is it just my usual forensic curiosity that brings me here, the unquenchable desire I've always had to somehow penetrate the mysteries of the human body? There is no way of integrating the mystery of death into things because dead equals gone; so birth really does feel like the best thing in terms of an opportunity to get in close to what makes us human, to peer between the cracks. Or am I here for another reason? Is this my own surgical way of reclaiming something, of proving to myself that I have returned to being the woman who is on the doing, and not the done-to, side of the feminist Rubicon?

I stand behind her slim back and see the spinal go in and play with switching, hologram-like, between knowing this is another person, and imagining her back as my own. I see the nurse erect the same screen, a cotton gown hooked between two drip stands at bosom height, to protect her and her husband from the sight that I was also shielded from, but this time have full access to. I remember the exact feeling of lying down on my back and looking up at the blank expanse of that screen, of not being able to move my legs or body. The voices around the room, the sense of absolute help-lessness. And against that, I feel the full status of my current position, standing and chatting to Ms P, the surgeon, aligning myself to her professionally by asking about the arcane specifics of the incision. Pfannenstiel? No, modified Joel-Cohen.

Ms P paints on chlorhexidine and measures two finger breadths above the pubis with her slim hand. There is the customary surprise of the first incision which never fails to gladden me. Outside in, it says, to reality. Red line, yellow fat, muscle and then Ms P puts down her knife to take the rectus muscles in her hands and heave them apart. The silvery peritoneum, rounded by pregnancy, peeps through like a child-drawn cloud. Ms P cuts it and I am just thinking of what layer might come next when she delivers the first baby. I am so used to disease, so accustomed to the purpose of surgery being to remove illness, that this perfect baby, already wailing its first muted wail, takes me quite by surprise.

This is what happened to me, though I didn't see it. This is what my womb looked like. This is how my girls were born, though they are unlikely to ever witness it. This is exactly how Ms P lifted my first twin up to the sky for me to see, before handing her over to the waiting nurse. This is what it was like to be a patient lying on exactly that bed, giving birth to twins, and this is what it's like to stand in my customary position, with the next important moment of the operation opening in front of me like a seam.

But all my feminist gymnastics – my attempts to fathom how we women must flip dextrously and repeatedly between being the subjects, the agents of our own fortunes, and the objects, the ones upon whom life is enacted – now stop. For next comes a marvel that goes beyond thought.

Ms P puts her hands into the woman's pelvis, into this red cavern of womb and gently, into the sunny operating theatre, as if it were a nest of precious eggs, brings up into the air, out of redness, a perfect, luminous, gleaming sphere. This is the second baby's amniotic sac, perfectly intact, raised like a crystal ball. The surface seems to spin and shine like the rainbow colours in oil that might lie in a thin layer on the surface of the sea, or in the curved rainbow of a bubble. And within this bubble, I can distinctly see the whorled pattern of the baby's head, the baby still floating and swimming in her quiet sea home.

Ms P lowers the screen so the parents can see. Everyone in theatre says ooooh, the staff allowing themselves a moment of pure vocalised wonder. It is here, in her hands, held aloft in the sun, a baby who is born and not yet born. It is a moment to stare right into, to look beyond, when time seems to stop, in which it feels like the truth is revealing itself. And then, aaaah, everyone says, as the bubble bursts and a perfect baby, the second twin, is lifted up to grasp the very first moment of her life.

Consult an anatomy book and you might be forgiven for thinking the uterus is a simple organ, a dull little triangle of flesh. Such descriptions rarely capture its dynamic nature, its potential size and scope or the variousness of how it manifests itself. They don't convey what it's like to dim the lights and peer at a uterus through a hysteroscope, a pot-holer wandering through a spooky cave dense with fibroids, or how it feels to cut one out to protect a woman from disease or, more dramatically still, to see one be transplanted into another woman's pelvis.

And no amount of watching can come close to the experience of actually having a womb, a properly felt sensation that begins with one's first period, repeats itself for a quarter of the weeks of one's reproductive life and develops through however many pregnancies and childbirths are encountered thereafter. What does it feel like to have kidneys? Like nothing really. How does it feel to have a brain? Like an abstract notion that there is something important inside my head. What about a womb? Mine bleeds like a flood and yours might ache until you faint. When you get pregnant, it will fill up your body and life. If you're lucky, it will bring you joy. During birth, you'll witness how it's strong enough to do the most important job a person is capable of it, whether you want it to or not. This hurts like hell so might be worth blanking with drugs if you're like me, or welcoming as a spiritual journey if you are someone else altogether. And, I have no doubt that there is a womb-ache sharp as any heartache felt by some so coldly described by doctors as nulliparous. And a fury felt in the belly of those women who never wanted babies at all, if only everyone else would shut up about it.

Ultimately though, what the womb gives each woman goes far beyond any children she might bear from it. Whether through monthly periods, the tectonics of pregnancy and childbirth, or the slow seasons of puberty, fertility and menopause, this organ requires a woman to exist in a constantly adapting relationship with her own body and the world. And if this makes the womb a burden, it is surely also a prism, granting us extraordinary imaginative reach. Is this part of what it is to be a woman, this profound repeated lesson in being cleaved from oneself? And if so, does the womb not equip us beautifully to grasp early and head-on what all adults must learn sooner or later, that the way our identity is tethered to our physical being is much more slippery than we might like to imagine, that the integrity of self is a kind of dream-state from which any of us might be rudely awakened at any moment, and with no warning?

4 November 2023

The cardiologist says sorry your screen is blank, the computer camera isn't working. I try to come across as calm and doctorly, but am distracted by the clinic Zoom timer counting down the eight remaining minutes of my appointment. He goes through a few things my palpitations might represent – two minutes left now – orders tests and adds something about me being a model patient. I look at the symptom diary I've kept for a month and wonder if there's a way to tell him about just one of them, though I don't really know how to describe it. 'It's like a fish flip-flopping inside of my chest,' I imagine myself saying.

Lungs

I lower my face to blue. Up close, the sea breaks against the rocks, foam splitting into diamonds. The sound of my own breath coming in and out of my snorkel is amplified, like wind in a tunnel. I glance up to reorient myself in the objective world. It's breezy, the sea ruffled and black. The boat is out to my right with Albert – who calls himself Jungle – at the helm while, to my left, the Caribbean mountain which nearly killed my father a few years ago bisects the landscape. I look up to its highest peak then down again, noticing how outside grey cliff becomes underwater blue cliff, stretching away darkly into the distance.

A good doctor needs bifocal vision. You have to marshal the generalities of anatomy, physiology and pathology, while remaining alive to the specific ways in which each sick patient deviates from the paradigm, since these are the details which might unlock a mysterious diagnosis, or direct treatment one way instead of another. For me, though, connecting the universal and particular truths of the human body has always been more than a clinical duty. It's the necessary step towards unlocking my passion. The margins of my textbooks are strewn with gossip. Because, however devoted I am to science, the only way I can breathe life into it is by making it personal. Here's what I mean.

My father sets his heart on the big mountain. The hotel staff try to dissuade him. It's nothing to do with his age, they say, the piton is simply too steep, fit only for professional climbers with ropes and crampons. Why doesn't he try the smaller slope? It's not to be scoffed at and will take a whole morning to trek up and down.

In the local town, he pays a man to escort him. There is a forty-five-year difference in their ages. My dad wears strong boots, carries water and a camera in a small backpack. They drive to the foot of the piton and begin their ascent before seven in the morning, just as the sun is rising. They have to use hands and feet from the outset and are soon breathing heavily.

The lungs are cone-shaped structures, surrounded by a lining called the pleura, encased within the bony ribcage. The right one has three lobes and is short to make room for the liver below it. The left has two lobes and is narrow so the heart can snuggle alongside it. People often think of the lungs like empty balloons, which inflate when we breathe in. In fact, when you cut one open, you don't find thin air at all, but dense, spongy tissue formed almost entirely of airways and blood vessels. Their thick origins – two main bronchi which arise from where the windpipe splits, plus right and left pulmonary arteries – enter each lung at a central hub called the hilum. Both types of tube then divide continually within the substance of the lung, like interwoven branches against a winter sky, from trunk to tiniest twig.

Airways terminate in grape-like clusters called alveoli. There are hundreds of these in the lungs, each one a circle of individual cells, where gas exchange takes place. Tiny capillaries filled with blood embrace each alveolus, the barrier between air and blood at this level gossamer-thin, comprising nothing more than a single layer of alveolar cells, a membrane and a single layer of capillary cells.

Inhale. This is the effortful part of breathing. You don't just pour air into your lungs like water into a glass. The respiratory pump, a collective term for the muscles of the shoulder girdle, diaphragm and inter-costals, actively contracts to expand the chest cavity.

Adding oomph are the pleura, adherent on one side to the lung and on the other to the chest wall. Negative pressure within the pleural space helps suck air into the nose and mouth and all the way down into the alveoli.

With each breath, a grapefruit-sized gulp of air enters our lungs – trillions of molecules. Most of it is nitrogen, with only about a fifth accounted for by oxygen in a very specific form, two atoms bound together. This O_2 is different to the more stable version found in the water molecules in our body, so highly reactive that we can inhale only small amounts at a time. On reaching the alveolus, it crosses the small distance into the capillary and then hooks on to a protein in the blood called haemoglobin. Oxygenated blood passes into the pulmonary veins and travels to the heart before being pumped all around the body. Once inside cells, O_2 is smashed into its constituent atoms, and either used right there or repurposed.

Exhale. This requires no effort and is simply the result of the respiratory pump relaxing. Carbon dioxide passes out of the body in the opposite direction to oxygen coming in, diffusing easily out of the blood from capillary to alveolus and then travelling up through the airways. When it reaches the nose and mouth, CO_2 is blown back into the atmosphere.

*

Eyes on hands and feet. Know-how from marathon days. Time climb with breathing. Keep rhythm with pull and clamber. Homage to mountaineers in thin air. Hats off to freedivers under weight of water. Sometimes they pause, and the guide points something out in passing. This plant with waxy bright red flowers? The Ginger Lily. That trunk adorned with prickles just up ahead? The Ouch-ouch Tree, also known as Monkey-Don't-Climb.

The last stretch nearly takes his breath away. There is a mango tree with a knotted rope hanging from a branch to shimmy up because the rock there is vertical; a narrow ledge he has to squeeze along sideways, with nothing in front but empty space; the awkward delight of standing next to a stranger on top of the world. His escort tells him he's the oldest person ever to climb this piton. But he is already smiling at the somewhere point far below where he imagines my mum must be. She puts her book on the sand and emerges from under the bleached grass parasol, looks up to find the peak. He is at its highest point now, eyes turned down to receive her gaze.

When all is well, we don't even think about breathing. This isn't so for all mammals. Bottlenose dolphins make a conscious decision to rise to the surface eight to twelve times a minute and use a blowhole. This creates an obvious problem when they are sleeping, for which they have evolved an ingenious solution. One half of the dolphin's brain, plus the eye on the opposite side of the head, shuts down. The remaining hemisphere and contralateral eye maintain a low level of alertness, watching out for predators and obstacles, prompting the dolphin to surface and take a breath. After two hours on duty, the sides of the brain and eyes swap.

We humans need some say in our respiration because we have to coordinate it with other things we do: speak, laugh, cough, vomit, cry and sing. Signals from motor and premotor areas of the brain help us orchestrate this stuff, travelling down to the muscles of respiration in what are called pyramidal tracts. But our small trick of self-control is nothing compared to the complicated chemical and neurological network which automatically governs respiration.

The brainstem joins the brain to the spinal cord and is built, from top to bottom, of mid-brain, pons and medulla. The last two are crucial to breathing, responding to information received from stretch receptors in the lungs as well as the ever-changing chemistry of the blood. The pneumotaxic centre in the pons, for example, controls the rhythm of our breath, its delicate interplay between in and out. Damage here can cause something called apneustic breathing, where a person inhales abnormally for whole minutes at a time before exhalation takes over.

It's all downhill now. He thinks he has the knack of swinging out into a half-abseil, feet flat on the rock face. But the rope is thin and greasy. When his boot slips, his grip isn't enough. The drop feels endless. Orange nylon scorches his hands until he is forced to let go. For a while, he feels only free air all around him. Then comes a hard landing. As he falls down the mountain, he senses something essential is leaving him – Sanskrit *atman*, Hebrew *ruach*, Greek *pneuma* – his spirit, his life. He stops sharp and sudden against a rock and cannot catch his breath.

He sees his own panic reflected in the guide, oh man oh man, red T-shirt dipping in and out of the trees. But he feels it inside his chest, an indescribable pain. Just moving forwards is suffocating. After many hours, they reach level ground and find the van. The makeshift hospital is located in a football stadium. In X-ray, the doctor tells him he has six broken ribs, a collapsed lung and a chest full of blood.

He braces himself as the medic unsheathes the weapon necessary for his cure, a silicone tube as thick as a finger, with a long metal spike on one end. He thinks he might pass out as the sharp trocar is pushed between two ribs in the vulnerable area around the side of his chest. The doctor connects the tube to a large bottle which immediately fills with blood. He sees my mum at the entrance to the ward, and breathes a deep sigh of relief.

The lungs are life's bookends. A baby cries and we welcome them into the world. A loved one breathes their last and we know they're gone forever. Foetal lung buds develop at five weeks' gestation, ten weeks later all the main airways have formed and, in the last third of pregnancy, these septate into millions of little bronchioles and alveoli. Normal foetal lungs are waterlogged but, at birth, this changes. When the baby pushes its way out, chemoreceptors register low oxygen, information they communicate to the brain. Clamping of the umbilical cord blocks placental factors that were inhibiting breathing. The baby starts to wail, causing intrathoracic pressure to rise, which keeps the alveoli open. Any remaining lung fluid is then forced into the capillaries and lymphatic circulation.

As we approach death, our dry lungs get wet again. Secretions accumulate and are hard to clear because of a weakened cough and swallowing reflex. Characteristic patterns emerge. Cheyne–Stokes breathing involves a cycle of periods of hyperventilation, followed by those in which no breathing occurs at all, as the body tries unsuccessfully to regulate its carbon dioxide levels. And in the very last stages of life there may be agonal breathing, when a person sighs or gasps as their brainstem tries in vain to correct falling oxygen.

My husband and the rest of the snorkellers are way ahead, distant as bath toys. I came here to see the place my dad nearly died a few years back, but it's time to get on with my own holiday. Kicking off, I pass coral which resembles the body, yellow tubes and brown petals like genitals and huge brainy spheres. I inhale deeply and duck down, freed from weighty subjectivity by the brief suspension of my own breath sounds. A porcupine fish stares out from baleful eyes. An octopus slithers its legs back under a rock. Soon, my chest is tight, sending me up among striped clouds of Sergeant Majors, through three dimensions of blue. With my last puff, I blow a jet of spume from my snorkel, before filling my lungs again with bright, clean air.

Before my father fell off that mountain, I never stopped to imagine what it would be like to gasp for air, to literally fear you might suffocate. It took hearing his story to animate facts which had previously been abstract. But there's a world of difference between what happened to my dad, a free man with an over-weening sense of adventure on a luxury winter break in the Caribbean, and the circumstances in which most others end up mortally breathless. Dyspnoea – the word doctors use to distinguish pathological short-ness of breath from the kind fit people experience on exertion – may be the unifying symptom of every lung disease and trauma. But it doesn't fall equally on all sectors of the population.

At the extreme end, breathlessness hits those in war zones, with chemical weapons specifically designed to target the respiratory system employed since early history. Peloponnesian forces released sulphur fumes in the town of Plataea in 479 BC, and the army of Leo IX of Byzantium threw vases filled with quicklime, overpowering their enemy when they smashed. At the Battle of Ypres, the German army released 168 tonnes of chlorine gas towards the Allied trenches. French and Algerian soldiers didn't know what had hit them and, within moments, 1,100 were dead and 7,000 injured. The British added phosgene and mustard gas to their toxic arsenal in retaliation and, by the end of the First World War, chemical agents had collectively wounded or killed around a million.

The litany goes on. Mussolini dropped mustard gas on Ethiopia in 1936, and the Nazis used gas on a scale not seen before or since in their concentration camps. The US army deployed napalm and Agent Orange in the Vietnam War, and Egypt used mustard gas in Yemen in 1963. Iraq wielded chemical weapons against Iran in the 1980s, and the Syrian regime has serially employed sarin and chlorine to subdue its own citizens. More than fifty different chemical weapons with various sinister mechanisms for damaging the lungs are currently stockpiled. Nerve agents like sarin, tabun and soman cause respiratory muscles to stop working by interfering with normal signals at the neuromuscular junction. Choking agents cause pulmonary oedema, a process in which fluid leaves the lung tissue and enters the air spaces, effectively drowning its victims. International laws to prohibit their use have been ineffectual, and perhaps it's no wonder. What more terrifying assault could there be than one which threatens a person's ability to draw breath?

It's natural to feel outrage at these atrocities, but we shouldn't kid ourselves. For even in peacetime, there's a clear apartheid between those who breathe easily and those who can't. Just look at chronic obstructive pulmonary disease (COPD), the commonest cause of breathlessness globally. Ninety per cent of fatalities from this inflammatory condition occur in low-income countries. And in the so-called developed world, where it is ranked the fourth-biggest killer, with 3.7 million affected in the UK alone, COPD is concentrated disproportionately among ethnic minorities and lower socioeconomic groups. As doctors, we're taught to think about the aetiology of symptoms along strictly pathological lines, as if it's our organs' fault when we get sick. But what about the environmental circumstances that give rise to these bodily failures? It's starkly obvious – not just in the case of COPD but asthma, lung cancer, heart failure and, most recently, Covid – that lung diseases aren't randomly allocated across society, and neither are the conditions which give rise to them.

Smoking remains the main risk factor for dyspnoea, and it's worth unpicking why this toxic habit remains so much more prevalent among the disadvantaged, cigarettes perhaps providing an easy hit to those with more life stressors and fewer alternatives for pleasure. But the other big cause of breathlessness, poor-quality air, is even harder to avoid. We should have learned our lesson from the Great Smog of 1952, when a deadly combination of windless weather and a rise in coal emissions resulted in the death from asphyxiation of 12,000 people in London. No such luck. There are still

40,000 avoidable deaths from air pollution every year in the UK. Traffic fumes may be the chief culprit but, as Sadiq Khan's book *Breathe* reminds us, poor people bear the brunt, since they're more likely than the wealthy to live and work in uncongenial areas.

But breathlessness isn't just the literal consequence of inhaling bad air. A startling number of the world's crises are manifested by this organ. Another group of migrants dies in the back of a lorry from asphyxiation. A four-year-old boy washes up dead on a beach in Greece, his lungs full of seawater. George Floyd lies on a road suffocating, with a policeman kneeling on his neck, while he begs, 'I can't breathe.' Respiration is a political as well as a physiological act, our capacity to perform it not just a sign of life, but of freedom.

The lungs bring some of our most intense personal experiences. The tight anxious breathing of madness and grief. The deep lungful of air that gives succour at the end of a long period of confinement. The gulping of a sob, the paroxysm of laughter. The mounting breaths of sex, the sustained exhalation against a closed glottis that pushes a baby into the world.

But these organs also connect us, at the most basic atomic level, via the air we breathe. What does the Hippocratic Oath really amount to if all it demands of a doctor is an intention to do no harm?

Our duty should include bearing witness to the often intolerable lives our patients describe, lives they must return to, as well as holding the government to account for condemning some citizens to languish while others prosper. With a problem as big as breathlessness, we're going to need all sorts of solutions. The only way we'll arrive at them is by thinking outside the box.

At the Royal Brompton Hospital, doctors are trying out a new therapy. Most respiratory diseases restrict lung volume, but in emphysema, the opposite is the case. Chronic inflammation demolishes the walls between alveoli, replacing useful tissue with redundant air spaces called bullae. Patients end up with huge, stiff lungs and difficulty breathing. Bronchoscopic lung reduction aims to ease matters, not by expanding the lungs but by making them smaller, thereby optimising the mechanics of respiration.

There are precedents in medical history. Before antibiotics came on the scene, patients with tuberculosis often spent years in a sanatorium, not just taking the air, but being subjected to all sorts of unpleasant surgical procedures, whose shared purpose was to decrease the bulk of unhealthy lung tissue. Artificial pneumothorax, where the lung was collapsed on purpose, thoracoplasty in which ribs were removed, and plombage, which involved inserting rubber or even ping-pong balls into the lungs to cause fibrosis, were all commonplace at the beginning of the twentieth century.

In the pristine bronchoscopy suite, the consultant brings a CT scan up on the screen and shows me the huge black spaces that yawn where healthy lung parenchyma should be. Just a couple of feet away, the patient lies asleep on his back, a long history of COPD evident in his barrel chest. He's tried everything, the doctor tells me, hasn't smoked in years, is fastidious about his lung rehab, and uses inhalers. But, aged just seventy, he's permanently breathless, can't climb stairs and is reliant on home oxygen.

The bronchoscope looks slender as a drinking straw entering the patient's lips, then ginormous a couple of seconds later when it reappears on the monitor, the internal landscape of the patient's airways beautifully magnified. Soft cushion of mouth gives way to trachea, with its helter-skelter of cartilaginous rings and, as the consultant reaches the broad ridge of the carina, I find myself leaning slightly as he angles the camera into the left main bronchus. As the scope weaves its way down towards the target lobe, I lose my bearings, but he soon reorientates me, so that I see the way segmental airways split at multiple junctions, their lumens magnified, pink and pulsing with the transmitted movement of the heart.

And now it's time to deflate the lobe. The consultant holds the tip of his catheter still and, pressing a button with his thumb, releases a tiny silicone valve, which wedges itself into the bifurcation of two airways. I notice its little duckbill, which opens and closes, letting air out from the lung with each of the patient's exhalations but not allowing any back in. Once several valves are in place, this part of the lung will empty and collapse. Some take a few days to adjust, but often the effect is immediate, he says. Wait for the anaesthetic to wear off and you'll probably see this patient take the best breath he's had in years.

On the other side of the hospital, Ed tunes his guitar as his singers start to arrive. Some bring in fresh air on their coats, while others come straight from the ward. A man in a wheelchair pulls a drip-stand alongside him, while a woman brings in a paint-chipped oxygen canister on a trolley. Most of the oldies have COPD, though other lung diseases are represented too: cystic fibrosis, cancer, bronchiectasis, long Covid. What everyone has in common is breathlessness. You can hear it in the coughing and wheezing. You can see it in the silent greetings, just a smile, nod or squeeze of the arm, as people find their seats.

Once we're settled, Ed invites those who can to get up. Stand tall and proud, pull your shoulders back, he says, inhale. Feel the expanse across your chest and belly, make space. Singing isn't about who has the most breath, but how you control it. Loosen your faces, waggle your tongues, come on you lot, give me a shhhhh, and ooooh and, all together now, a loud shout of hey!

He passes out sheets of music, strums a few chords and begins to guide us through Perry Como's 'Magic Moments'. Everyone knows the tune but there is nothing lazy about how we're allowed to sing it. He points out exactly where the breaths should be taken and, like the proud conductor of a serious choir, is punctilious about technique. I'm amazed by how ambitious some of the phrases are and how ably many in the group can manage them. After a few passes all the way through, everyone bursts into applause before Ed strikes up again, with the intro to Simon and Garfunkel's 'Bridge Over Troubled Water'.

Once considered unorthodox, Singing for Breathing – run by the Royal Brompton and Harefield Arts team – has now been rolled out across more than fifty hospitals in the UK. Randomised controlled trials have helped win approval from the British Lung Foundation, proving singing to be at least as effective as more traditional lung physiotherapy in dyspnoeic patients. But the benefits aren't just felt in the lungs. All too frequently, people with respiratory disease encounter high rates of anxiety, low mood and social isolation. In a 2016 survey of group singing, patients unanimously reported not only an improvement in their breathing, but also in their overall quality of life, sense of well-being and social-connectedness. Doctors often dismiss qualitative research as unscientific, but the connection between subjective experience and function couldn't be clearer than it is here, in this room.

As we draw to the end of the song, and Ed plays the last bars that the strings would usually carry, I look around the group. The singers look different, shoulders relaxed, faces open, interactions for which there was no breath a short hour ago now possible. And when I close my eyes, blocking out the clinical paraphernalia that declares these individuals as respiratory patients, I notice something else. The wheezing is quieter, there are fewer coughs than before. All I can hear is the sound of a group of people who have chosen to come together and enjoy each other's company, the music of conversation and laughter.

*

At the Scripps Institution of Oceanography in California, Ralph Keeling is close to a diagnosis. Analysing daily air samples collected from geochemical stations all over the world, he's spent his whole career compiling an accurate record of how global oxygen levels vary within a single day, seasonally and across history. And a clear pattern is revealing itself.

It turns out there is much less variability between world locations than you might expect. Whether he reaches for the sample from Hawaii or Canada or Antarctica first, it's all the same. Oxygen levels rise during the day, when plants and microbes become active, and drop at night. With the sun as pacemaker, they wax in summer and wane in winter. He loves the way this looks on a graph, the regularity of the oscillations. More concerning is the other line, whose downward trend shows the gradual decline in oxygen over time, a counterpoint to the rising levels of carbon dioxide his late father, Charles Keeling, spent his lifetime recording.

People often say his dad's Keeling Curve was what finally proved the connection between human activity, rising carbon dioxide levels and climate change. He knows his own research has been important too. So, if he occasionally becomes frustrated by the repetitiveness of the sampling, or how slow people are to

ALIVE

react to their geochemical findings, he has only to remember sitting at the kitchen table with his father all those years ago, and the conversation they had, which revealed to him what his life's work would be. He still believes that tiny discoveries, properly communicated, can have global consequences. And watching the NASA timelapse now, with its beautiful shadows of oxygen and carbon dioxide rising and falling daily, he feels hopeful. It isn't too late. There's everything to play for. Just look, it's like the whole world's breathing.

Skin

I bring my knife to his throat. Against the collar of green drape, under the silver illumination of the operating light, my patient's skin looks brightly detailed. Tan from summer and with a sheen of chlorhexidine, goose-bumped by nervousness and plump from the local I've just injected. I pause momentarily, blade resting on the line I've drawn in purple felt-tip. Am I certain? Yes, I cut.

Most operations start with a skin incision. In the early years of my training, I assumed the jolt I experienced as I watched consecutive bosses make that first peachy slit was pure exhilaration. Decades after taking the knife in my own hand, I know there's more to it. Like at the theatre when – as the curtains go up – you get a flash of the almost silly artifice of the thing, a first incision marks something true, but that we'd rather not dwell on. Your skin is all that holds you. It defines where you end and the world begins. Everything inside your skin is you. Everything outside it is not-you. This isn't just any old bit of anatomy then. It's the big daddy, the meta-organ, without which all the others would literally fall apart.

Let's step back now from the high emotion of the operating table. I want to reassure you that, outside of these sharp surgical circumstances, your skin is up to the job it's tasked with. When you consider it contains heat, water and a thousand different chemicals, while simultaneously protecting you against sunshine, allergens and irritants, infections and trauma, it's clear this is no mean feat. So, what is the envelope of our selves actually made of? Secretly, I've always pictured the skin as a cake with two sponges and icing between them. But this won't do for proper science. What does the microscope reveal?

The skin has three layers: the epidermis, the basement membrane and the dermis. The epidermis is on the outside, the bit we face the world with. It varies in thickness across the body, from the leathery millimetre which gloves the palms of the hands and soles of the feet, to a tenth that calibre on the eyelids. Bare of blood vessels, the epidermis comprises several substrata with lovely memorable names, the horny one at the top, and the granular, prickle and basal layers lying sequentially below.

The basal layer is a single sheet of columnar cells.

In a continuing cycle of thirty to sixty days, new cells form here then migrate up, getting flatter and flatter as they go. By the time they reach the surface, most have become keratinocytes, mini armour plates packed tightly against the world with its endless assaults. But the epidermis isn't a simple seal. A variety of cell types are dotted through it, each with its own defensive part to play. Stem cells make new basal cells if the current ones are destroyed. Melanocytes produce the protective pigment melanin. Merkel cells provide information by interpreting feelings of fine touch. And Langerhans cells assist in immune defence. A brief glimpse at a scenario we've all become familiar with shows what these guys get up to.

You're at the basin, working your hands into a bubbly lather for the umpteenth time today. First off, soap comes into contact with the top layer of your skin, which includes a few Langerhans cells. These are shaped like starfish, and their snaggy arms catch any irritant soap molecules that pass by. Hugging the rogues, Langerhans cells swim back upstream, through the prickle and basal layers of the epidermis into the dermis, and hop, damaging cargo and all, into the lymphatic system. Here, they quickly re-dress the soap molecules in a new costume that will be easily recognised by T-cells, which – spurred to action – do two things.

They produce leucocytes, which engulf and destroy the antigens, in this scenario the soap molecules. They also spawn clones, which are primed against a future soapy assailant. Any subsequent assault will trigger inflammation, that protective process we recognise as redness, soreness and swelling after multiple episodes of washing our hands.

But where were we? The epidermis sits atop the hefty dermis. Its main ingredient is collagen, that bouncy protein which keeps our flesh nubile, and becomes tatty as we age. The dermis contains other proteins too, as well as water and a material called ground substance which acts as a shock absorber. And woven through it all are erector pili, the muscle which gives us goosebumps, blood vessels to help regulate temperature, lymphatics to drain infection, a bunch of immune cells and about a million nerves, most of which are concentrated in the face and extremities.

Last is the basement membrane. Returning to my cake analogy, this equals the icing between the two sponges. Its trick of welding the skin together is reinforced by the physical fact of the epidermis and dermis nestling in hillocks against each other. You can see this undulating design in the whorls of your fingertips.

Sometimes it takes a disease to make anatomy memorable. Epidermolysis bullosa (EB) perfectly illustrates that, without all three layers, our skin is cat-astrophically compromised. The consequence of a fault in the gene which encodes collagen 7, a protein essen-tial to the architecture of the basement membrane, this rare condition causes profound suffering. Even gentle physical contact shears epidermis against dermis, resulting in the formation of blisters all over the body. Chronic scarring makes patients' fingers and toes amal-gamate into useless stumps. And the pain is said to be like that of third-degree burns. Research – which involves harvesting a tiny bit of affected skin, infiltrat-ing it with the correct collagen 7 gene and growing it out in the lab, before regrafting it – is offering real hope to patients with this incurable condition, but the work is still in its early stages.

Decades ago, I was summoned to clinic, one of a rowdy gang of medical students, to meet a patient with EB. This young man's appointment was already underway when we arrived, his mother painstak-ingly removing dressings from every part of his body, a twice-daily ritual for them. I'll never forget how awful it felt to stand in that room while the consult-ant chivvied those at the back to get closer for a good look, the young man's quiet endurance, the excruciat-ing intimacy of his mother's touch, perhaps the only kind he would ever know.

But shame, and a realisation of the special privilege of moving through the world oblivious of one's own skin, weren't the only things I took away that day. I also learned something fundamental about disease in general, and the skin in particular. Only part of what EB patients suffer is a result of the error in their anatomy. Yes, the pain and blisters come from a faulty basement membrane. But the rest, the scarring and disability, arise out of the body's pathological attempt to compensate. In EB, the skin tries to correct its inherent flimsiness by growing tough tissue that is impossibly tight and inflexible. It turns out that an absolute frontier is as undesirable as no frontier. Healthy skin isn't a barrier at all, but a delicate semi-permeable membrane. Our soft and vulnerable selves may need protection. But we also have to remain open.

I turn my key quietly in the lock. Inside, I dump my bag and hospital ID, before slipping upstairs, fast as a snake. I know they'll be asleep, but it doesn't matter. I push the door open gently, hear the carpet brush against its underside. Sneak in, shut the door behind me, and inhale deeply. Skin of baby twins. Perfect sweet alloy of nappy and sweat.

Developing skin is so fragile. At four weeks' gestation, it's a mere single cell thick. In the second month, nerve endings begin to develop, followed by the first tufting of hair and nails. Pigmentation gets going at around four months, and sweat glands a few weeks after that. Even after birth, a baby's skin is like gossamer: it contains little water, the network of blood vessels is rudimentary, and the concentration of melanin low. With an immature microbiome and a less acidic pH than that of an adult, baby skin is particularly susceptible to infection.

With so little of its armamentarium up and running, what is there to insulate a baby's tender skin from the harshness of the outside world? The answer is human touch. Science plainly shows the benefit to newborn infants of early skin-to-skin contact, sometimes known as kangaroo mother care. It stabilises their temperature, breathing, heart rate and blood pressure, regulates blood sugar levels, and helps a good skin flora to establish. It decreases crying and pain, as well as fosters a strong baby-to-parent bond. A century ago, Freud insisted that an individual's early sensory experiences of their own skin were crucial to the development of a healthy ego. And though he's out of fashion now, developmental psychologists continue to explore the psychic importance of early parental touch. It's as if this loving embrace provides the ideal level of containment for a child's soft subjectivity to flourish in.

Of course, when I enter my babies' room, none of this crosses my mind. I'm not here for facts, but because I am addicted. I lean over each of their cots in turn and press my skin to theirs, testing out how much sniffing, snuffling, stroking, squeezing and kissing I can pull off without waking them up. I am like Kevin Kline in *A Fish Called Wanda* when he breathes deeply into Jamie Lee Curtis's boot. I am nearly cross-eyed with delight, and with a sort of relief. They are alive. I am home. Whatever transgression I may have committed with my foray out into the workplace and the world, all is still as it should be.

If I have any thoughts in the silent paradise of this small bedroom, they relate to time. Look how they are growing. They used to be tiny as dolls. If they carry on this fast, they'll be teenagers tomorrow and I will be ancient. Develop quickly babies and give me some peace. Never grow another inch.

Spread out on the grass like parachute silk, your skin would cover more than two square metres. Why is its surface area so huge? To enable the easy passage of two essential things, heat and sunlight. The first law of thermodynamics states energy has to go somewhere. Most of the calories we consume, as fuel for the multiple physiological reactions that keep us alive, are eventually released as heat. The hottest organs are the liver, brain, heart and muscles, but all warmth gets dispersed around the body by the blood and ends up escaping through the skin.

The human body is amazingly good at keeping its core temperature stable, between 36.1 and 37.2 degrees Celsius to be exact. If it's cold out, we conserve heat by shivering and constricting our surface blood vessels, to divert warmth inwards. As the ambient temperature rises, the opposite occurs, blood vessels dilating to allow heat to exit the body, mainly through radiation or convection. If it gets really sweltering, especially above 35 degrees, the skin has another trick. Sweat glands kick into action, squeezing out droplets of water, which evaporate and cool us down.

As heat goes out, so sun comes in. Sunlight helps lower blood pressure, as well as boost good sleep and mood, but the main reason we need it is for vitamin D. Vitamin D regulates calcium and phosphate, minerals essential for healthy bones and teeth. Even little kids can tell you this. But it does other things too, supporting our nervous and immune systems, muscles and brain, and helping prevent diabetes, multiple sclerosis and even some cancers. Some of this important substance can be sourced from food like oily fish, meat, eggs and cheese, but most of what we need comes from ultraviolet rays hitting our skin.

At medical school, we memorised the three stages by which sunlight becomes vitamin D. Keratinocytes in the epidermis turn it into a biologically inert form of vitamin D called cholecalciferol. Then, in a further two steps, the liver and kidneys conjure the metabolically active 1,25 dihydroxyvitamin D, or calcitriol. But no one tests me on biochemistry anymore, so I'm free to kick back and wonder. Look at our human skin, how the things that cross its frontier gesture to both our smallness and grandeur. On the one hand, the way we make heat – those of us who live in ease, at least – has become ever more insular. We traipse from TV to kitchen cupboard, or call Deliveroo, barely reaching out an arm's length for the fuel we need. And yet, our primal requirement for sunshine forces us to continue turning outwards towards the universe. We may want to keep ourselves to ourselves, but the truth is that we can't survive without succour from something so distant as to be almost abstract, a star nearly 100 million miles away.

The big children's doors are closed. My daughter has painted her name on hers. My son's is a collage of skateboarding stickers. There's no red sign out debarring entry. But the message from both quarters couldn't be clearer. Don't come in. Don't even get close. Out of self-preservation, then, I consider adolescent skin only in the most general sense: the loss of peachy smoothness, the strange new eccrine smells, the increased production of sebum, the arrival of new hair. Acne vulgaris just around the corner, or a metal allergy to accompany the piercing of those perfect lobules. Or perhaps even some squeal-inducing infestations on the horizon to go with bad sexual choices.

I miss the physical closeness I had with these two when they were small, who now bend their bodies away from mine when I hug them. But the lack of information is worse. What are they thinking and feeling? Are they OK? If there was a problem, would I have any idea, when I'm kept so much in the dark? But, hark. The noise of floorboards creaking, the approach of sweaty feet. I creep away quickly before getting busted leaning into their rooms, trying to divine something about who my children are becoming.

Melanoma is the deadliest form of skin cancer. It occurs when too much exposure to the sun triggers mutations in the DNA of a person's melanocytes, and the development of tumours. Alarmingly, this kind of cancer is doubling every ten years in the UK, faster than any other malignancy except lung cancer in women. One of the scary things about melanoma is how hard it hits the young. The average age of diagnosis is fifty-seven years old, and more than three quarters occur in those under seventy. The other is how vulnerable we are: just one or two episodes of severe sunburn in childhood are enough to double one's lifelong risk.

I've seen a child under ten with melanoma. I've operated on a man in his twenties with one on his leg so advanced that by the time he came in to see me with his mother, it had lost all of its black pigment and was a large, wet tumour. I also saw a young woman recently, who walked into clinic sporting a mahogany tan plus two separate melanomas, a toxic combo achieved by the melanin tablets she'd bought over the internet in combination with a sunbed. Sadly, even patients like this are often flabbergasted to hear that the mole they admit has been growing and changing right in front of their eyes is cancer. The skin seems so far from the organs which power life, the heart and the brain. How is it possible, you can see them wondering, for something so shallow to matter so much? How could what looks like no more than a surface stain have the potential to kill them?

Superficial spreading melanoma is the commonest

type. Lentigo maligna melanoma affects the elderly and is often slow to develop. Acral lentiginous melanoma is a sneaky one which occurs on the palms of the hands and soles of the feet. Nodular melanoma is the worst and appears as a mole that you could feel with your finger even in the dark. Though these tumours vary in aggressiveness, some metastasising within a just a few weeks, a basic pattern of spread is shared by all of them, which first enlarge horizontally, before extending down into the dermis, and then seeding into local lymph nodes and distant organs. So on the off-chance it may encourage a single individual with a dodgy mole to go to their GP, let me say this: if you have any mark on your skin that stands out from the others, or has got bigger, changed colour or become weird in any way, please get your doctor to look at it. It might save your life.

You can see why dermatologists get worked up. I know one who says that every single photon of light poses a threat to one's health, and that the only safe sunscreen is a house. But this is an extreme view. Most skin cancers can be avoided with a balanced approach and sensible amount of sun exposure. And, mercifully, the vast majority of them aren't melanomas.

People are sometimes surprised to hear that dermatologists go through the same intensive medical training as other physicians. The skin has been so successfully co-opted by the cosmetics industry that we're more likely to think of it as a site for obsessive self-improvement than survival. But this is the organ where our deepest selves and the outside world meet. All manner of issues get imprinted on its canvas.

There are no signs to Colnbrook Immigration Removal Centre. After circling the roundabouts near Heathrow, I slow to ask a couple of guys working on the road the way, then spot it, an anonymous block surrounded by high fencing, with coils of barbed wire on the top.

Reception is small and unlovely, empty but for a water machine, a tattered poster warning about the penalties of taking in contraband and a plaque advertising the security company in charge, one of several such units that doesn't have the dubious credentials of being state-run. From a small hatch, the receptionist clocks my NHS badge and checks something on his screen. Then he ushers me through a door, on the other side of which waits the GP I'm shadowing today.

We head along corridors, doors are unlocked for us and, at last, we are shown into a small room with a barred window, a table and chairs. We sit with our backs to the door, facing the empty seat on the other side. The GP asks the guard to leave the room, before unpacking from her bag a notebook and pencil, ruler and tape measure, and a small camera. She lays these things on the table.

I look down at my hands in the dim light, my wedding ring, my skin against the cuff of my shirt, and see for the first time how much even this tiny snapshot of my body expresses about my fortunate place in the world. I picture all the internal boundaries contained inside this one, the epithelia that hold my muscles and bones and blood vessels in place, the membranes that separate not just my vital organs, but the cells they're made from, the ever-smaller borders that split cells into molecules, molecules into atoms, atoms into the sub-atomic particles from which everything in the universe is made.

Then I scope outwards, imagining the frontiers that lie just beyond the boundary of myself, the parochial lines I cross in an average week, the thresholds in my home, between house and garden, room and spacious room. The small spaces I reach across to touch my loved ones, children, siblings, parents, husband. The familiar neighbourhood journeys, to a café, the super-market, my children's school. The visit in a warm car, through the outskirts of London to a safe district general hospital, into the operating theatre and out, and back home again. I am a white, middle-class doctor and can go where I like.

I don't know much about the man we are about to meet. Only that his skin has had to defend him against worse assaults than I've ever known. The journey he's made has been difficult and dangerous. He has passed through countries, crossing many borders to get here, knowing surely that he would not escape this, would become one of the 30,000 people who are detained indefinitely in our country every year, in a place that feels like prison, waiting for an asylum claim to be processed, or to be sent back home. The story he will tell us is of trauma and torture and escape. But as he enters the room, an interpreter on one side and guard on the other, he knows full well that his account alone won't be enough, that words are flimsy symbols in this bid for freedom.

The only thing that might save him is the graphic story written on his skin. We will measure and itemise his scars, giving our medical opinion on whether what he has described is clinically plausible, whether the mechanism of action he reports is consistent with the precise state of healing, the shape and depth and pattern of each dermal injury. He steps into the room, and the GP turns and holds out her hand. Maybe the marks beneath his clothes will be bad enough to help us write a report that will stand up in court. Perhaps there is a chance for healing. And one day soon, might he even begin to know what I have taken for granted all my life, the comfort of living peacefully in one's own skin?

Through the kitchen window, I spy my parents at the bottom of the garden. In the amber afternoon, my mum lies reading in her favourite deckchair, its vibrant stripes now faded. On each shin, I can just make out the scars from her recent surgery, the excision of a couple of minor skin cancers. A few feet away, my dad leans over to inspect his beehives and stands up again, back towards me. From this distance, there is little to give away his eighty years, or all that he's lived through. Unbent, unbald, still strong, he could pass for sixty. His sole stigma of age is hidden beneath his clothing, where my dad's epidermis confounds his youthful bearing. A genetic predisposition to overproduce growth factors in the skin, responding to even the friction of clothes and towels day after day, has culminated in a map of senescence. Hundreds of benign seborrhoeic keratoses populate his slender trunk. Some are small and pale like freckles while others, the size of ten-pence coins, have the dark texture of rhino hide. In the spaces in between, tiny scarlet haemangiomas called Campbell de Morgan spots spray his skin, as if his grandchildren had chased him around, flicking him with the red paint from the tips of their brushes.

If in doubt, cut it out. There have been great leaps in the medical management of melanoma, with immunotherapy targeting specific gene mutations and viral vectors being used to destroy tumour cells. The life expectancy of people with advanced disease has been dramatically extended by these advances. But the mainstay of treatment is still surgery. And so it is that I sit each week, in a little operating theatre adjoining clinic, while my dermatology colleagues scrutinise suspicious skin lesions with their dermatoscopes, and send along any that look malignant for an immediate biopsy or excision.

This isn't just to get cancer out of the body pronto, but also to provide a tissue sample for the pathologist. The treacherous potential of a mole is worked out using something called an ocular micrometer, which measures its Breslow thickness, the vertical distance between the granular layer and the deepest part of the tumour. If you can catch a melanoma before it's a millimetre deep, the outlook is really good. When it's gone further, something called a sentinel node biopsy is performed: the area near the mole is injected with a dye to make the nearest lymph node light up. Then this node is biopsied, to work out if the melanoma has spread.

Despite training in ENT, I spend most of my operating time doing skin-cancer surgery these days. Melanomas may be the most serious, but other types of tumour are often bigger and more surgically challenging. Squamous cell carcinomas, or 'squames', as we matily refer to them among ourselves, occur when sunlight causes a mutation in the p53 tumour suppression gene. Keratinocytes then start producing keratin in an uncontrolled way and the resulting tumours may extend to many centimetres in diameter, standing proud to the skin like a volcano or even with the exploded appearance of a volcano which has erupted. They can also spread around the body. Basal cell carcinomas, historically called rodent ulcers because they have the gnawed appearance of something a hungry rat might have sunk its teeth into, are the commonest skin cancers of all. They don't spread, but often crop up on the face which can make for tricky surgery.

You have to be careful not to look too keen when you have a knife in your hand. I know that excising skin cancers isn't exactly high-drama surgery. It certainly isn't what I dreamed of as a young trainee. But year after year, I still enjoy it. Partly this is because treating cancer feels important. The cutting may be small, but the result is life-saving. The rest of the pleasure comes from the craft of the surgery itself. In most parts of the body, a mole is excised and the resulting hole, what we call the surgical defect, is closed with one straight line. But operating on the face is best. This is where real skill is needed to get a good cosmetic result. Elderly patients are easy because they have looser skin to play with. The neck, the sides of the face and the temples are pretty forgiving too. If you cut through the lips, it's essential to line up the vermilion borders perfectly when sewing the edges back together. Under the eyes, you need to angle your incision with care to avoid drooping called ectropion. The nose is damn painful to inject, and has to be considered in its cosmetic subunits, which are the little areas which you shouldn't cross with your knife if you want things to look pretty afterwards. The ear is great fun to operate on, but bleeds like buggery.

One of my favourite operations is called wedge excision of the ear. You start by drawing a triangle around the cancer in the shape of a pizza slice – imagine the crust of your wedge as the rim of the ear and its floppy, tomatoey point nearer the ear hole. Then with two crunchy-sounding snips with strong, straight-bladed scissors, you cut the wedge out, cancer embedded in it. When you've stemmed the bleeding, you bring the two sides together and stitch the back and the front of the ear up, making sure to get all the curly bits of the pinna to match each other. Amazingly, you can take out quite a big bite and, though the ear looks a little shortened, it doesn't lose any of its intricate shape.

It's also satisfying thinking of what to do when removing a cancer from someone's face leaves a hole too big to be closed by simply bringing the two sides together. Then you have to be creative and patch things up either with a skin graft or something called a flap. Skin grafts to cover holes in the face are typically taken from behind the ear or above the clavicle. You harvest a patch which goes all the way through to the dermis but with as little fat on it as possible, and attach it to its new home with tiny stitches. By the time the stitches come out, the graft should be nice and pink, having picked up its new blood supply.

Flaps are bits of skin which you rotate from one position in the face into another. There's a lovely one that works on the nose called a bilobed flap, which looks like a three-leafed clover, and another called an advancement flap which is the shape of the letter H, especially useful for cancers on the forehead. There's usually a point when someone's face is wide open and bleeding, and you don't quite know how it's all going to come together again. But the end result is like slotting in the final piece in a wooden Wentworth jigsaw puzzle, click-clack, incredibly satisfying. And the cosmetic results can be quite beautiful.

Brushing our teeth side by side, my husband and I could be a pathology exhibit of middle-aged skin. Resolutely handsome, his epidermis is nonetheless in a terrible state after six decades of life, many lived under the glare of the Australian sun. Hairs sprout unruly across his shoulders. Pillowcase-white beneath his towel, his broad back looks as if it belongs to a different person. A chaos of sun damage, solar lentigenes and naevi of many shades form countries and continents, their surface as textured as an ordnance survey map. He's not alone. By sixty, we can all expect the degeneration of collagen and elastin in the dermis, and hormonal changes which will cause atrophy. There will be sagging and deep wrinkling. Photodamage will manifest itself as elastosis and liver spots. Our nail growth will slow, our hair will get thin and grey because of a depletion in melanocytes in the hair bulb and outer root sheath. With that beautiful combination of self-regard and lack of it, which is the inheritance of men, my spouse does not care a wit about any of this. His mind is else-where. He doesn't even see himself.

And as for me, I observe new signs of decrepitude

every day. When I run, my flesh takes a couple of seconds to slump into position, as if chasing the rest of my body. All once-perky parts hang inches lower than they used to, and deep rhytids crease my cheeks. Do I feel rueful about this? Perhaps a little. Mainly, though, I wonder why on earth, when there are a thousand painful, suppurating, itchy, weeping, purulent, disfiguring and even lethal skin conditions out there, those of us lucky enough to have functioning skin, that does a grand job, get so exercised just because it happens to be ageing?

But who am I to moralise? I count the folk whose skin comes within my immediate caring remit, not just my patients but my family too. My velvety parents, their friends all dead or dying. My rough-skinned husband, as he heads towards old age, lighting the way just in front of me. My adolescent son and daughter, their cutaneous dramas recalling the glorious rampages of my own younger life, still memorable but long gone. My toddlers' delectable skin, which reminds me how sweet my bigger kids once were. What a luxury this great epidermal map is that I find myself at the heart of. But the skin is also an interface. Mine may separate me from the outside world but is also the membrane through which I experience it. Your skin may allow you to keep your distance, but it also invites me to reach out and touch you.

11 January 2024

Hello. I had a call from Prof. A weeks ago saying my echo shows significant worsening and that he needs to discuss my case urgently at the MDT. Please can you let me know if this has happened or when it will happen as I'm keen to know what changes have occurred and what the treatment plan will be.

Hi. I'm afraid there's a long list of patients waiting. We aim to discuss your case in the next 6-8 weeks. Once you've been discussed, one of the team will call you with the outcome and you will also receive a letter. All the best.

Please can I have a copy of my recent echo report in the meantime?

I'm afraid that hasn't yet been finalised on the system.

167

Breast

It's possible you've never thought of the breasts as organs. Maybe it's their external position that throws you, something about the way they point out to the world as well as inwards to the more private space of biology? Or perhaps they just don't seem that interesting?

I get it. The archetypal, pre-childbearing adult breast is pretty rudimentary. Made of a circular body and axillary tail, each one consists of little more than fifteen to twenty glandular lobes arranged within a background of fat. Shaped like bunches of grapes, and filled with units called alveoli where milk is produced, lobes drain into ducts, which exit at the nipple. The nipple and areola are reinforced with contractile muscle, and the latter is dotted with glands called Montgomery's tubercles. The breast gets its blood from axillary, internal thoracic and intercostal arteries, and drains to the corresponding veins. Lymph goes to the nodes in the armpit, and the nerve supply comes from the fourth to sixth intercostals. And there it is, you might think, everything you need to know about this organ, wrapped up in a single paragraph.

Not so. By pinning the breast down like a butterfly, freeze-framing just one moment in its lifespan, anatomy misses most of the juicy stuff. We ought to know better. As long ago as the early nineteenth century, Astley Cooper – physician to King George IV and Queen Victoria – sourced hundreds of breasts from corpses of different ages, painstakingly injecting their complex ductal systems with wax dyes and mercury to produce a set of crystalline galactograms, as beautiful as they are instructive, which exquisitely map the breast's structural diversity. I often get antsy about how many landmarks in the female body are named after men, but I certainly don't begrudge this tenacious explorer the Suspensory Ligaments of Astley Cooper that run like supportive wires through the mammary tissue, giving breasts their youthful perkiness. No one has done more to bring to life the distinct stages these organs progress through in a lifetime. Let's clip through them.

Breasts pop up in the womb. By six weeks' gestation, parallel milk lines have formed on each side of the torso, running southbound from neck to groin. Other mammals grow multiple pairs of teats along these lines, but people tend to get just two. In boys, the breast is held in a quiescent state by circulating testosterone. But by the time a girl is born, she already has an intricate tree-like configuration of ducts and lobules embedded in the tissue beneath her nipple. Occasionally, female babies' breasts even produce a little milk at birth in response to maternal oestrogen, a phenomenon which – in the die-hard tradition of demonising females for their biology – is known as witch's milk.

Usually, though, the breast lies low until puberty. Then a flare of oestrogen prompts that unsettling Lolita-like stage in a girl's life, when breast buds appear, signalling that the immature ducts and lobules are beginning to mature. Progesterone brings up the rear, increasing breast size by about thirteen per cent before each period, voluptuousness which is partly retained as each month passes. New breast tissue continues to amass like this for much longer than you might expect, not just during early adulthood, but until a woman reaches about thirty-five.

Puberty is occurring ever earlier in the Western world, which is worrying given that a woman's risk of developing breast cancer appears linked with how much oestrogen she is exposed to over a lifetime. What isn't clear is why this is happening. Is it just that our girls are chubbier than they used to be? Fat is sometimes referred to as the third ovary because it contains an enzyme called aromatase which converts cholesterol into oestrogen. A hormone called leptin – made in fat cells – may also be involved since a certain amount of it has to be made before puberty can start, and this threshold is reached earlier in overweight girls. Or perhaps it's something else altogether. Are we exposing our kids to too many harmful chemicals, some of which are attaching to oestrogen receptors in the breast and triggering precocious development?

Whatever the answer, puberty definitely isn't the breast's main game. The only organ in the entire body that doesn't automatically reach full maturity with adulthood, it takes special circumstances to trigger its prime. Linnaeus coined the word mammals in 1758 to group all creatures who breastfeed their young. But the label does more than celebrate a common nurturing activity. It shines the spotlight on the organ that does the feeding.

The lactating breast is a super-breast. And the way it gears up is nothing short of a virtuoso physiological performance. As pregnancy heads towards term, placental lactogen expands the nipple and areola into an unignorable baby-beacon. Progesterone holds all the eager milk-making apparatus in check before birth. Then levels of this hormone plummet as soon as the placenta is delivered, firing the starter gun. Prolactin now gets pulsed hourly through the bloodstream, while a set of other hormones mobilise all necessary ingredients needed for milk production from the mother's blood into the milk-making units of the breast, the alveoli. By this stage, the breasts have doubled in weight.

The final clarion call is when the newborn baby wails, or reaches for the nipple. At this moment, oxytocin triggers let-down, that curious, almost sexual, tingling which happens just before the muscles in the breast release a gush of milk into the baby's lusty mouth. From the modest 25 to 50 ml of colostrum made in the first few days after birth, the breasts' supply of mature milk soars to about 800 ml a day at six months. Mothers of twins generate twice this amount – I had to keep bumper bars of Cadbury's Fruit and Nut in my bedside table to scoff in the middle of the night when I was breastfeeding mine – and thin women produce about fifteen per cent more milk than their corpulent friends, to compensate for the relatively low-fat content of their supply. It's no wonder breastfeeding is so exhausting. Each energy-dense litre delivers 750 kcal to the growing baby, and making it expends thirty per cent of a woman's metabolic output, the equivalent of walking seven miles a day.

Physiology is so bright and exciting. It isn't afraid to get to grips with the human body as a living, breathing entity. So why does anatomy, by comparison, feel so inert? Of all the subjects a medical student is taught on the way to becoming a doctor, why does this one alone seem somehow beyond scrutiny, its lessons set in stone?

On the one hand, the answer is right there in the word. From the Greek *tomia*, 'to cut', and *ana* meaning 'up', anatomy has always been equated with dissection. The science may have flourished in those places and times when dissection was encouraged – like third-century BC Alexandria, when Greek physicians Herophilus and Erasistratus made huge strides in anatomy by taking apart the bodies of executed criminals. But it has also suffered long fallow periods, when a combination of the law, religion and social taboo conspired to shut the practice down. The longest stagnant spell was the Middle Ages, when scholars of the body relied entirely for their anatomical education on half-truths handed down in books written by predecessors like Aristotle and Galen.

But exposition isn't enough to guarantee truth. When Frederick II took the radical step of re-legalising dissection in 1231 for those intending to practise medicine, releasing the hungry young doctors of

the day on real cadavers after 1,700 years of prohib-
ition, he may have been making history. But the way
these biannual events were arranged was at odds with
genuine enquiry. A 'sector', often the local barber,
did the cutting. Next to him stood another stooge
called the 'ostensor', whose sole function was to point
in the direction of the body part being described. The
only one there with any knowledge was the 'lector'
but, thanks to his privileged status, he stood at a safe
distance from the smelly reality of the body, too far
away to actually see what he was describing, reading
facts from a book probably written by Galen. It's as if
these guys couldn't quite snap out of the passive style
of learning they'd grown up with, despite fresh meat.
The purpose of such formal sessions, which remind
me of my own anatomical education, wasn't to challenge the status quo or find new things, but to enshrine
and inculcate the so-called facts that had already been
established.

Dissection continued to spread across the universities of Europe during the thirteenth and fourteenth
centuries. But, to my mind, what really marked the
turning point between old casuistry and the explosion of new knowledge wasn't scientific scrutiny
so much as the opening up of the human body to a
brand new audience, whose eyes were untutored

enough to see things clearly. From about the mid fifteenth century, Renaissance artists like the Pollaiuolo
brothers, da Vinci and Michelangelo, keen to perfect
their creative representations of the human frame,
started to do their own dissections. The visual culture
of paintings, sculptures and lavish books that their
interest sparked, soon morphed into mass-produced
leaflets and widespread anatomical models called
écorchés and, over the next hundred years, common
interest in anatomy grew to such an extent that dissections were frequently performed to the public in
churches and large anatomy theatres across Padua,
Bologna, Leiden and Paris. The phrase *nosce te ipsum* –
'know thyself' – found everywhere in illustrations,
frontispieces of books and carved into the walls of
anatomy theatres of the day, captures the zeitgeist. By
the time Andreas Vesalius appeared in the sixteenth
century, with his clear mission statement that any
physician wanting to learn anatomy must be prepared
to personally dissect and explore the body, the old
rote-learning methods were damn near obsolete. His
1543 book, *De Humani Corporis Fabrica*, is famous for
showing that much of the anatomy that scholars had
believed for generations was wrong. But it wasn't just
radical for its facts. Published just twenty-four years
after da Vinci's death, this was the first medical text

to include really accurate images of the human body. Science had been transformed forever, by public interest and the arts.

Let art come to the rescue again! What better way could there be to bring myself back to the here and now, to shake myself from the constraints of a too-rigid anatomical education, than by going to see some paintings at the National Gallery. What jollier protest against the neutered depiction glaring out from my textbook, with its dull black-and-white diagram of a passive breast, stump of an arm pulled up to reveal the axillary tail and lymph nodes, a wedge cut out like a cake slice to offset the web of ducts within?

My bus rocks down the hill towards the river. I google 'the breast in art' on my phone and get this collage. Artefacts of women with giant breasts date back to the Stone Age. The fantasy of the multi-breasted woman is prominent in early Indian art and also in second-century AD statues of Artemis of Ephesus. The Greeks preferred to worship the phallus, associating the breast with the vicious Amazons. Images of breasts were suppressed by Catholicism for most of the Middle Ages, but in the Renaissance, the image of the Madonna breastfeeding the infant Jesus became de rigueur. The erotic breast burst forth in the fifteenth century in a portrait of Agnes Sorrel, the mistress of Charles VII. The eighteenth century saw the first depictions of the domestic breast, as contemporary medical and state opinion converged on the importance of breastfeeding. French Revolution art often featured the breast as a symbol of freedom, while the trend for seeing this organ as a sex object has continued to gain traction in art from the nineteenth century to the present day.

These facts reinforce what I was already thinking. Lactation may be the most important job breasts do, but it's not what they get attention for. Which woman hasn't heard the hollers? Get your tits out, jugs, hooters. We are sex objects before anything else. In parts of Africa and the South Pacific, females are free to walk around bare-chested without hassle, but this certainly isn't the case in our culture. Show us your melons, knockers, boobs. In public, a girl can barely think straight for the unwanted attention her breasts receive. Look at the pair on that, bazookas, rack. She's made to feel her paltry worth every time she sets foot outdoors. Combine this routine abusive scrutiny with the diet of cosmetically perfect breasts we're force-fed by our media, and is it any wonder so many young women grow up paranoid about how their bodies look, seeking perfection in a Barbie-like ideal that is found naturally in just one in 100,000 women?

According to a 2011 article in the *New York Times*, a whacking $820 million is spent globally on breast implants every year. The first such operation was done in 1895 by a German called Czerny, who removed a fatty tumour from a woman's buttock and placed it in her chest. All sorts of gruesome experiments followed with substances as diverse as glass, ivory, ox cartilage and paraffin, Teflon and Plexiglas, but it wasn't until silicone came on the scene that the boob job as we know it took off. In the years after the Second World War, this material wonderfully revolutionised the manufacture of medical supplies like catheters, stents and blood bags. Then, one day, a Texan plastic surgeon called Thomas Cronin had a creepy Eureka moment. Enjoying the delicious feel of a blood bag in his hand, he found himself dreaming of bigger and better things. A woman called Timmie Jean Lindsey, unsuspectingly visiting hospital in 1962 to have a tattoo removed, was persuaded by Cronin to become his first breast implant guinea pig in exchange for having her ears tucked back, and the false god of the silicone tit was enshrined.

I used to be terrified of science. I grew up knowing I was bad at it as clearly as I knew I was a girl. Years into my medical training, despite a growing bank of exams passed and skills mastered, I still fretted. Would I ever catch up? Was it really possible to become a doctor, with nothing more than a soft, arts-loving brain to assist me? What a load of rubbish that was. I know now that science is after the same truths as art. Physics is a language just like French is a language. Chemistry may be hard, but it isn't any harder than philosophy. The line between the two main disciplines is as silly as the Emperor's New Clothes. A child can't be bad at science any more than a child can be bad at life. I'd been missing out for years.

Physiology is the body in action. I love this science because, unlike anatomy, it doesn't shove its truths in your face, preferring to probe gently at why biological systems have the structures they do. It breathes life into how we understand the human organs, describing not just what they're made of, but what they are for. In the case of the breast, this is spectacular.

The breast turns blood into milk. It actually magics one life-giving bodily fluid into another. Picture the difference. Claret-red blood in a tube that your doctor has just drawn off. White milk in a baby's bottle. The overall gist of how this happens is that building blocks from the mother's blood exit through the wall of her lace-thin capillaries and are taken up by the alveoli and turned into milk there. But ellipsing in this way kills what's most interesting. The beauty is in the detail.

Glance at the lovely curved surface of the breast. Even the Montgomery's tubercles which dot the areola have a role. Past wisdom said these were sebaceous glands, providing lubrication to the nipples to help prevent cracking during breastfeeding. But it's clear now that some of them actually produce tiny amounts of milk. More of these tubercles are found in the upper lateral section of the areola, where a baby's nose is directed during breastfeeding, suggesting they may also be functioning as organs of scent. It's thought the higher the number of them a woman has, the more easily her baby will latch on.

But the real action takes place deep within the breast. So, come with me, through one of the holes in the nipple and along a milk duct. Burrow further through ever smaller ductules, until pop. We are inside an alveolus. This single milk-making unit is a circle of secretory cells – a fact discovered by my old friend Astley Cooper – surrounded by a layer of muscle. Imagine this circle as a wedding ring sitting on a finger. The side of the cells next to the finger is called the apex. The side of the cells next to the air is the basolateral side. The finger is the draining ductule, and the air is the extracellular space, through which run the maternal capillaries.

The first substance the breast sets about making after birth is colostrum. This requires the junctions between individual cells of the alveolar ring to be loose enough to let lots of stuff through, including sodium, potassium and chloride, protein and immune substances, and beta-carotene, which gives colostrum its jazzy yellow colour. What this baby appetiser doesn't have much of is fat and carbohydrate. A few days into a baby's life, the bonds between those little cells in the alveolus tighten up, and mature milk is produced, a rich and complex elixir whose vast array of constituents I can only touch on here.

Each of the dietary units in breast milk has a different recipe and is made from scratch. Take the example of lactose. This is milk's main carbohydrate and not only develops a baby's brain, but also works osmotically to pull water and minerals into the alveolar cells. Several steps are involved in its manufacture. First, glucose enters the basolateral membrane of the alveolus from the mother's blood. Some of it becomes galactose. Then, in a part of the cell called the Golgi apparatus, glucose and galactose undergo a chemical reaction which forms lactose. A breastfeeding mother can make this important sugar whether she is well nourished or not.

Protein also has to be made especially. Its two main components are casein and whey. Amino acids are deposited by the maternal blood and taken up through the basolateral membrane. Meanwhile, the nucleus of the alveolar cell makes a template out of something called mRNA which shows the amino acids how to assemble into proteins that the baby needs.

Fat contributes more calories to the growing child than anything else. Here, fatty acids and glycerol are dumped by maternal blood and taken up by the alveolus. They travel to another exotic-sounding place called the endoplasmic reticulum, where they are packaged into triglycerides. Then, as they push into the draining ductule, each fat globule is wrapped in little bit of cell membrane, like a piece of cling film, to stop them all coalescing.

If a mother is lucky enough to be well fed, milk fats come from her diet but, even when this isn't so, a woman's own adipose stores will be dissolved to provide for her baby. The alveolus alters fat concentrations across a single feed, with the hind milk having more than the foremilk. Fat levels in breastmilk also ebb and flow over the course of the day, falling to their lowest at night and peaking in the afternoon and early evening.

*

My bus corners the Embankment, the top deck flashing green as we clatter through trees, before trundling up towards Trafalgar Square. I think of the posh gym nearby that I used to visit when I cared more about appearances than I do now, the dolly women in the changing room, mirror-bound with their bald muffs, rigid breasts and waxy faces. I return to my phone screen. I've seen plenty of Madonna Lactans iconography over the years, the young Mary absolutely erect, one pale bosom freed from the tight band of her bodice to feed her child. Even in these pictures, it's as if the breast doesn't entirely belong to its owner, performing instead as a symbol. I want to get to grips with something real.

With each bump in the road, I feel my own breasts jolt. I put my right hand inside my coat and under my sweatshirt. My left bosom is warm and heavy. Despite peri-menopause, these organs are building themselves up against the faint possibility of a pregnancy and the need to feed a child. Then it comes, that dreamy, electrifying feeling I sometimes have when I'm thinking intently about the body, while simultaneously feeling aware of living inside one, making me believe it might be possible to fully see, at the same time as fully being. But pouf, and it's gone, and the old hiatus opens up again. My breasts are linked by their remarkable biology to all the others in the world, but they are also as familiar as old cushions. They are every-breasts. But they are also mine alone.

When I step off the bus and see that the National Portrait Gallery is in the final week of its annual competition show, I realise that it isn't the great masters down the road that I want to survey, lined up in their austere, wine-coloured halls. I'm after something more immediate. If anything can get to the heart of human identity, it's a portrait. With a quickening of my step, I wonder how many of this year's exhibits might feature breasts and, more importantly, what these paintings might have to tell me.

Inside, I find three portraits featuring naked breasts. The first one shows a modern-looking Eve in the Garden of Eden with almost photographic accuracy. She is depicted in profile with a short haircut, an impassive face and a perfect upturned tit. It reminds me of a 1980s Athena poster and doesn't stir me. In the next room, I come across a more interesting example. A woman stares out from the canvas. Only her top half is shown and she's bare, shielding one of her breasts with an arm. The information next to the picture tells me that the sitter is an artist herself, and the painter of this portrait is her friend. You can sense their comradeship in the unabashedness of her pose and the way she looks out. He has used egg tempera and every inch of the painstakingly layered canvas glows. Her breasts are given the same attention as her face, her eyes and her mouth and the picture hits you with a sense of this woman's individuality.

My first thought on finding the winning painting is what a coincidence it is to chance on this exhibition while investigating the breast and discover that the first prize has been given to a husband's oil painting of his wife breastfeeding. Hooray, I think. How nice to see a woman celebrated performing one of biology's most remarkable functions. And what a great counterpoint this intensely personal work of art is to the sterile diagram in my textbook.

The real brilliance of the picture takes longer to work on me. As I stand there, staring, straightforward approbation gives way to unease. Part of this comes from the perspective from which the breastfeeding woman has been painted. To get this view, the artist must have been standing while his subject sat, and it puts her at a disadvantage. There is also something aggressively unglamorous about the way he has depicted his wife, her absurdly pendulous breast with its vast areola half obscuring the baby's face, and ugly brown dressing gown hanging open. Presented like this, she seems imprisoned in her domesticity. It is impossible to imagine her out in the world feeding her baby in public in a park or café, let alone doing something else.

Breastfeeding is fraught. On the plus side, lots of women find it fulfilling, and there's no doubt about its nutritional and immune benefits. The WHO advises us to suckle our babies until they are at least two, and there are lactivist women everywhere, ready to harangue and browbeat those of us who can't or won't. But a woman must be tenacious to persist. A 2016 Department of Health study cited embarrassment as one of the main reasons women stop breastfeeding, and UNICEF has confirmed that only two per cent of women are still managing to feed their babies exclusively this way at six months. The media can't get enough of naked, nubile tits, but when a woman tries to do something useful with them, she's often met with disapproval. The clear cultural message seems to be that she should go home.

The painting I'm standing in front of supersedes argument. It brilliantly captures the contradictions of this still-political bodily function. It asks all the questions but suspends resolution. The mother looks subjugated and at the same time absolutely engaged in feeding her child. She is blissful, but trapped.

*

Much is made of the common ground between surgeons and artists. But, while any portraitist's gift resides in their ability to engage profoundly with a subject's identity, this humane concern is still sadly lacking in many of our operating theatres.

For the archetypal surgeon-villain, one need look no further than Ian Paterson, who must have started his training around the same time as I did and in 2017 received a twenty-year jail sentence for performing unnecessary breast surgery on hundreds of women. But the small-town examples chill me too, the ones whose failings go under the radar so that they are able to keep working. The most cack-handed, insensitive and dangerous surgeon I ever trained under was a breast surgeon. Sure, he was motivated to save lives, but he lacked even the most cursory regard for a woman's feelings.

I assisted in many of his mastectomies. I won't forget his habit of lobbing the breast he'd just sliced off across the operating table and into a kidney dish, like a baller shooting a basket. Nor how it felt to go with him afterwards to see a patient on the ward, the curtain bulging with all of us gathered round the bed, the rosiness of this consultant's triumph, the second smile of his mask-line still bisecting his handsome jowls, the tremulousness of whichever woman it happened to be that day, sitting in bed as he stood, looking up at him like a girl, flat-chested beneath her bandages, trying to meet her saviour in gratitude, no place to acknowledge that though he had given her something, he had taken something too and it wasn't just any lump of tissue, not the same as a stretch of bowel or a bit of spleen.

People say they're happy to forsake bedside manner for a surgeon with great hands. But we shouldn't set our sights so low. Everyone knows about the rocky history of cosmetic breast surgery, the earliest attempts often resulting in death, and modern implants beset with complications, leakage of carcinogen, scarring and rupture to name but a few. But there is a bigger truth. Problems will occur in any operating theatre where the person in charge doesn't give a shit about the individual lying on the table. And one of the commonest casualties of cavalier surgery is damage to a patient's nerve supply.

Breasts are a powerful erogenous zone. Their skin is served by anterior and cutaneous branches of the fourth to sixth intercostal nerves, the former doing most of the saucy work. I like to imagine it literally humming with sensory information. The areola is the most sensitive part and those of us who have small breasts are thought to get the most sexual pleasure from them. What a compensation prize! Curvy women might have the most crowd-pleasing breasts, but not the hottest ones. A functional MRI study done by the American psychologist Barry Komisaruk in 2011 showed that the three separate areas of the parietal cortex that light up when a woman's genitals are stimulated also flash when her breasts are touched. I don't just hate boob jobs because they're dangerous and foolish. I object to the fact that they put sexiness, appearance and performance in front of sexuality, sensation and experience. With surgical breast enhancement, a woman may gain the power to elicit male desire, but in so doing she relegates herself to the erotic sidelines.

But it's not all doom and gloom. At the Royal Marsden Hospital, Sutton, in a gleaming operating theatre, two young women consultants stand side by side at the table. They are part of the clinical army who treat the one in eight women in the UK who develops breast cancer, though what's happening in this room isn't the regular cut and thrust. Two weeks ago, using a needle, they planted a tiny magnetic seed in the centre of their patient's tumour. They want what cancer surgeons have always wanted, to cut out disease. But these women are focused on something else besides, the person who surrounds the tumour. They are determined to preserve as much of her normal breast as possible.

The gowned women wait, gloved hands crossed over their chest. The patient is wheeled in. One steps forwards silently and applies her probe to the woman lying beneath her, to her breast, watches the red digital numbers on her monitor, listens out for the tone whose frequency rises as she gets nearer to the epicentre of the tumour. She follows her signal with the blade, dissecting down with virtually no loss of blood to where the cancer is, cutting around it, lifting it out, smaller than a plum. The breast is still itself, a small incision in the side, barely any fullness lost, no noticeable change in its contour. The person with breast cancer never seemed to matter when I was training, but they do now. The surgeon works quietly and without bravura. Her hands are quick and neat.

But it's not just these young heroines with a job to do. Getting the breast out of the anatomical doldrums will take more than surgery, plus me banging my drum. It's time to challenge the fact that – regardless of whether we're being ogled, or disapproved of – our breasts are treated like public property. Let's stop colluding in the obsession with how these organs look, and start to focus more on, and maybe even celebrate, how they really feel.

Girlhood. I don't need science to tell me my breasts are linked to my genitals. All summer, a boy's hands come to rest there in the sunlight. Through my closed eyes, it's orange in the sun and wind, and there is no fear in me at all and nothing I want more than his hands on this part of me. We should announce the breast as the emblem of our own pleasure. We should be teaching our girls in school that their desire matters too and the breasts offer a simple route to sexual joy that won't harm them.

Early motherhood. I am a new milk-cow, encased in a scaffolding bra. Cabbage wilts on my scorching chest. My baby does nothing but cry to be fed, then feeds and vomits, before the whole cycle starts again. It is always night-time with no one else around. Then again: I arrive from a gum-tree Australian summer into snowy Heathrow, alone with my baby. Home is cold so we go straight to bed. Over the edge of the podgy duvet, the room is blue-quiet, the window framing a three-dimensional puzzle of snow. She feeds quietly, her hand like a star against my heart and I know I won't forget this happiness as long as I live.

Older motherhood. Wise as a fox, I am wheeled down the corridor to the ward, while a nurse on either side of me crams a twin's tiny face into each breast. Their little mouths bang against me comically, but I am not a bit concerned because I am too happy that they have been born safely and are well. Later, my nipples will bleed and my toes curl, but it is excellent to be an old mother. I drink one of the little bottles of champagne from my mum and know that, though I am starting again, it will all be over soon enough. Fireworks crackle in the November sky and I hold my last two babies close. It is a beginning and an end.

Now. The children are noisy in the garden, but they are far enough away, and it is quiet up here. I take my top off and unclip my bra. I place my clothes on top of the toilet and stand head-on in front of the mirror. My heyday is over, these breasts have no more amazing and feeding to do, but they still matter to me. I inspect them one by one, the nipples and areolae then the rest, raising my arms up and putting them down again to check for skin puckering. I step into the bath, lower myself holding onto the sides, lean back and watch the shiny heat encase my goose-bumped bareness. Pressing my spine into the bottom of the bath to get my chest under the surface, I begin with my left breast. Soft as marshmallow in the water, I start to feel it with my right hand, just as I was taught. Three fingers together, starting at the nipple and exploring the flesh in circles, ever wider and firmer. Trying to find anything odd, heart ready at any moment to thump in underwater alarm. There isn't much ground to cover and I finish by putting my left arm down, making a warm wet hollow of my armpit which I push my fingers into, searching for lymph nodes, before moving to the other side of my body.

Then I am done and there is still time. I let in more hot water from the tap and lie back, pondering the strange, unbridgeable gap that exists between the body science describes and the one each of us is living inside right this moment. I look along the length of my body in the steam. Feet and legs and pubes and stomach and breasts. I'm middle-aged but still happy naked. I press down into the warmth and, feeling the water close above me, I settle into the absolute silence of myself.

Kidney

There's no one around so I duck behind a bush and drop my jeans, feel the chill of winter on my arse before the hot relief of peeing after the long drive. In this position, Jo Shapcott's poem 'Piss Flower' comes to mind and I briefly imagine rising forty feet high on my own proud fountain of urine. But the sign outside the building across the car park – Greenview Renal Unit – reminds me of my more prosaic purpose. I've come to spend a few days observing dialysis. I'm tired of the expert view. I want to change things up a bit and spend some time just hanging out with a patient. What's it like, I wonder, living life in the shadow of a disease?

I text the nurse in charge from the waiting room. A plastic Christmas tree blinks in the corner and a sign peeling from the window reminds staff to turn the lights out before leaving. Soon, the internal door clicks open and Mel ushers me down the corridor. There are fifty-two main renal units in the UK – she turns back while walking – each with a handful of satellites like this, so patients can get their treatment locally. Most visit on alternate days, for several hours per session. Three groups can be squeezed in each day just so long as a tight schedule is maintained. The doors are open from 6.30 a.m. to 10.30 p.m. except Sundays and Christmas.

We enter the room and everyone looks up. A digital clock the size of a sports banner hangs above the nurses' station. Twelve beds are arranged against the walls in a horseshoe shape and they're all occupied, but it's impossible to see the patients, so bundled up are they in coats, blankets, hats and scarves. The only bits of body I can make out are single, bare arms which protrude from the swaddles, connecting their inhabitants via bright red cords to the machines which stand at each bedside, humming loudly, implacable as Daleks.

Those of us lucky enough to have two functioning kidneys barely give them a second thought. Tucked away at the back of the abdomen in an area called the retroperitoneum, these fist-sized viscera are impossible to feel in one's own body and even doctors struggle to palpate them. But don't be fooled. The kidneys might be smooth operators, but they're working harder than any other organ, a truth proved by the fact they receive a quarter of all the blood leaving the heart. What keeps them so busy? They regulate blood pressure by balancing water and salt. They make vitamin D and a hormone called erythropoietin, which prompts the birth of new red blood cells. Most importantly, they clean the blood. It might seem a leisurely task. After all, we pee only a few times a day, releasing a maximum of two litres of urine. But this scant effluent masks a great efficiency. The actual volume of blood entering your kidneys is staggering – 200 litres every twenty-four hours – it's just that we never see the ninety-nine per cent of it that gets reabsorbed there.

This brisk blood flow through your kidneys is what enables them to react, second by second, to the body's ever-changing homeostatic requirements. Inside your kidneys right now, a sophisticated calibration of fluid and other chemicals is taking place within 2 million subunits called nephrons, each too tiny for the eye to see. Renal physiology is damn tricky – there's a reason kidney doctors are so clever – but, as a surgeon, I've no choice but to keep things simple. So make a fist with your right hand, clasp it in your left, and imagine you're looking down at a single nephron.

Your left hand represents the glomerulus, a tuft of capillaries where blood entering from the renal artery gets sieved. Big molecules like proteins and blood cells can't squeeze through the little holes in the glomerulus, but all the smaller constituents of our blood pass into the Bowman's capsule, your right hand for now. From here, filtered blood enters the renal tubule, your right arm. Over its snaky course, water, minerals and salts get balanced out and, by the end of it, the nephron has reabsorbed what the body needs back into the bloodstream, while releasing toxins and excess water as urine.

68,000 people in the UK can't take this aspect of their physiology for granted, though. These patients have established renal failure, which is the polite way of saying kidney disease that isn't ever going to get better. Most is the result of diabetes or high blood pressure, but there are other causes too, some that you're born with, others that crop up later. What all of them share is needing either a transplant or regular dialysis to survive and, while it's a common misconception that kidney transplant provides a cure, the truth is much starker. Yes, it gives the best results – sixty per cent normal renal function compared to the much lower ten per cent restored by dialysis – but the blunt reality is that neither treatment can reverse the underlying cause of a patient's disease.

Mel takes me over to meet Lisa, and I am immediately drawn in by the silent clinical dance which has become second nature for them. First, Lisa removes coat and shoes, and gets on the scales. Mel notes her weight down on a clipboard, then taps numbers into the dialysis monitor which, she tells me, instructs the machine as to today's target, to remove four litres of fluid from the patient at a flow rate of 380 ml per minute. Lisa climbs into bed, coiling a scarf round her neck, pulling on a woolly hat and arranging a blanket around her knees. By the time Mel has unwrapped two needles, Lisa has already rolled up her sleeve and stretched out her arm, in the crook of which is the raised, blue swelling of her fistula.

I lean in and Mel pauses, needle in hand. Dialysis replaces what would normally be done by the kidney. But because the machine is way too bulky to fit inside the patient's body, their blood has to be drained out and circulated through the machine. It isn't like you or me having a blood test once in a blue moon. In this single dialysis session, Lisa's entire circulation will cycle continually between her body and the machine, which puts her vessels under great strain. The fistula – fashioned by a surgeon cutting open and connecting an artery and vein in the arm – provides a robust conduit between patient and machine. High-pressure flow from the artery makes the vein expand and toughen and, after a few weeks of maturing, it's fit for purpose. A good fistula sits proud from the skin like a tree root,

Mel says, resting her finger there. It buzzes when you press it.

She wipes Lisa's arm with chlorhexidine, pushes in one needle then another, and checks the patient details correspond with those on the side of the dialysate bag, before pressing a button which starts this fluid running through the filter. With a flick of another switch, bright red blood appears in one of the lines, chasing itself along the tubing until woman and machine are joined in one crimson loop. On the screen next to me, a pie chart timing this session shows a slice of white against a circle of blue.

Mel heads off to settle in her next patient and I am suddenly self-conscious. It's strange to be at a patient's bedside without a doctor's job to do, and I'm relieved when Lisa starts pointing out all the different parts of the machine. Here's the down-limb which carries the blood needing dialysis, that's the place heparin is added to keep it running smoothly, and there is the up-limb, which returns the filtered blood. She shows me the little bubble trap it has to pass through to make sure no air gets in, and I peer inside where what looks like a simple glass cylinder reveals itself to be no empty vessel at all, but a collection of thousands of hollow tubes containing Lisa's blood, with clear fluid around them. The tubes are perforated, she tells me, and it's through the holes that the process of dialysis takes place.

I'm busy pondering the strangely intimate relationship Lisa has with this machine, which seems almost like an extension of herself – do dialysis patients have a different sense of space than the rest of us? – when Mel puts a cup of tea on the table next to me. She's got a blanket too, and it's only when she wraps this round Lisa's shoulders that I realise she must have been shivering all this time. Dialysis works best when the blood is cooled to about 36 degrees, Mel explains. The first thing it does is remove the fluid a patient can't pee out anymore. The hydrostatic pressure of the blood being pumped through the machine pushes excess water out of the blood and into the dialysis fluid. Patients are weighed at the start of their session and, depending on how much fluid they need to dump, they're given a 'strong', 'medium' or a 'weak' bag of dialysate. Glucose is the thing that dictates this, pulling water osmotically into the 'container' of the dialysate. The second function of dialysis is clearance. Waste substances such as urea and creatinine pass osmotically from the patient's blood into the dialysis fluid. And the same principle is used to get substances into the blood. For example, if a patient is short of calcium, it can be added to the dialysate bag and will diffuse into the patient's circulation.

The sky through the slatted blinds changes from purple to grey. I go for a pee, and marvel at the feeling of a nagging bladder and the sight of a strong yellow ribbon of urine hitting the bowl. Checking my phone, I'm surprised to discover I've only been at Greenview three hours. I take my leave, saying I'll be back for Lisa's next session in a couple of days and step out from the static heat of the unit. The air is damp and salty, the sky yellow and the fields bare and wide. On the main road, I put my foot down and lean into roundabouts which follow fast on each other like cogs in a wheel, revelling in my day opening up in front of me. It's only when I pull up outside my B&B, switch off the engine and look out through the windscreen at the sea, where the spray is lifting off the crest of each peachy wave, that it strikes me I've learned almost nothing about Lisa.

Doctors aren't always good communicators. Is this a hangover from the paternalistic days when consultants told their patients what to do? Perhaps the kind of geeky kids who get into medical school aren't hot on people skills. Or maybe the problem just comes with the territory, and anyone would find it tricky talking to strangers about heavy stuff like life and death. Whatever you believe, research clearly shows that communication problems lie at the heart of the majority of patient complaints and litigation. As a result, formal training in this area has become compulsory for all medical students.

What an excellent development! Back when I was in training, consultant orders were to be followed, and any young surgeon caught doing something as outlandish as soliciting a patient's opinion on their own body or treatment plan would have been told to bugger off and become a GP. Nowadays, doctors are expected to collaborate with, rather than dictate to, those in their care, and all sorts of tools are available to help us learn how best to navigate the therapeutic relationship. The 2001 Kalamazoo Consensus Statement, for example, lays out a clear set of steps that can be applied to any clinical consultation – build a relationship, open the discussion, gather information, understand the patient perspective, share information, reach agreement on problems and plans, and provide closure – a recipe many courses promulgate through a mixture of observation and role-play exercises. And this is all to the good. What makes me sceptical isn't the noble ambition of communication-skills courses, but whether any of them actually achieve what they set out to do.

Judging by the available evidence, this form of education just isn't that successful. In post-course self-assessments, student doctors often report a sharpening of their own interpersonal skills, but such views rarely tally with those of an objective patient-assessor. Even verifiable improvements in empathy observed among doctors during a course appear to fade fast on their return to work. Perhaps most damning of all, a 2021 Cochrane review which looked at ninety different communication-skills courses – involving 10,124 students from the US, Europe, the Middle East and Asia – concluded that any beneficial effects were small and short-lived. The problem isn't just that the leisurely setting in which communication skills tend to be taught bears little relation to the high-stress clinical workplace. It turns out communication skills are very hard to teach. The didactic methods that work perfectly well for demonstrating how to take blood or use a stethoscope aren't easily transferable to the more nuanced arena of interpersonal relations. And this shouldn't surprise us. Communication is an art, not a science. And like any other form of creativity, it requires special conditions in which to flourish.

Born in the Netherlands in 1911, Willem Kolff was dyslexic as a child, but it didn't stop him getting into medical school nor hamper his native lust for invention. His first device, a cuff that aided the circulation of blood by inflating and deflating, was dreamt up while working as an anatomy assistant at Leiden University. When he qualified as a doctor and one of his first young patients died of kidney failure, it seemed the natural next step to try and come up with a mechanical way of replacing what the kidney did.

He was building on a body of research. At the end of the nineteenth century, Thomas Graham had invented something called a bell dialyser, a jar containing distilled water with an ox bladder suspended inside it. When Graham filled the bladder with urine and left it for a few hours, then removed the bladder and heated the jar until the distilled water dried out, he discovered sodium chloride and urea – the main components of urine – left at its base, having passed through the bladder by osmosis. Adolph Fick took things a step further by replacing the bladder with a more sophisticated collodion membrane made from cotton treated with chemicals, and managed to separate low molecular weight solutes from blood through it. And in 1924, Georg Haas was first to try dialysis on a human, though his patient survived for only fifteen minutes.

Though Kolff's first dialysis machine was a triumph of creative thinking – conjured from orange-juice cans, parts of a Ford water pump, sausage skins and an immersion bath – for two years, all sixteen of the patients he used it on died. But in 1945, his tenacity finally paid off when a woman who had been in a uraemic coma was revived after eleven hours by one of his artificial kidneys. There is a clip of Kolff online reporting how, when she opened her eyes, her first words were, 'I'm going to divorce my husband,' which she did, surviving another seven years.

After the end of the war, Kolff donated five of his machines to hospitals around the world, inviting anyone with something to contribute to help him improve the basic prototype. This led to important developments in the 1940s and 50s, including the creation of a vertical stationary drum with dialysate circulating around it, and the application of hydrostatic pressure, enabling excess water to be more easily removed from a patient's blood. But this isn't all Kolff achieved. He created the first blood bank in Europe in 1940. He developed the heart-lung machine for use in cardiac surgery as well as the first artificial heart. He contributed to research on artificial arms and ears and – aged eighty-eight – created the very first artificial eye. Kolff never named any of these devices after himself.

No individual in history has contributed more to the development of artificial organs than Willem Kolff. And yet dialysis machines have barely evolved at all in the past fifty years. Why not, you might ask? Where are the budding medical inventors of today? Let me put this question in return. Where would Kolff be now, if he were starting out in our modern NHS? Being hammered in a double-booked clinic, that's where, or wasting his time doing admin on a computer, his best thoughts scrambled. For all our technical advances, there is no opportunity in the UK for doctors to think creatively anymore.

Wednesday is a cold day of sharp colours. I go for a run on the beach, in the great bowl of sky and sea. The wind stings my ears and pins my body to the vast blueness like a kite and, though I barely make any progress, it feels amazing just to have a body that works, astonishing how, with no conscious input, my kidneys continue with their life-saving, full-time job, filtering and reabsorbing until they push out that perfect cocktail of creatinine and urea and water and ammonia, keeping back all that they need to make my body function smoothly. When I arrive at Greenview a little later with my notebook in hand, it's with a simple intention: to stay with Lisa for the duration of her dialysis session, and simply listen.

There's nothing she hasn't tried. Peritoneal dialysis came first. The cupboard under her stairs was piled high with boxes of dialysate. They put a tube in her abdomen, and she would pour in two litres of fluid, leave them for two hours, drain the whole lot out and down the loo, then repeat the rigmarole four times a day. It was nice to be at home but made her feel bloated. This was followed by a trial of overnight dialysis with a machine in the bedroom. The freedom was great, but it didn't filter enough out and was noisy. Next her mum donated a kidney, which didn't go as planned. She took months to recover, had to take steroids, hated getting fat, got tons of infections as well as diarrhoea from the anti-rejection drugs and was always at the hospital. Six years later, the transplant degenerated then failed. She still feels terrible about it, the fact there are three useless kidneys sitting in her abdominal cavity right now, none of them working. Her brother wants her to have one of his, but she can't face it, there's too much at stake, and she prefers the predictability of dialysis. The real challenge isn't the dialysis itself but what goes with it: her bones and teeth are rubbish because of renal bone disease, twice-weekly EPO injections hurt and the diet is miserable. She can't have anything with too much potassium, that's bananas and most fruit and veg, so she's always constipated. She can eat mash because the boiled water washes away the potassium, but not chips. A monthly baked potato is a treat. She has to avoid phosphate too, that's most dairy. Daily phosphate binders taste awful. It'd be fine to gorge on cakes but she doesn't like them. Worst of all is the fluid restriction, a maximum of one litre a day. In summer, she relies on ice cubes and sweets. She doesn't take holidays because the insurance is so high and arranging dialysis somewhere else too hard. Her son lives with his dad. She feels much better after dialysis though very tired and cold.

When I sit at my desk later and look at my notes, I'm struck by how different they are from what I usually write down when talking to a patient, less orderly for sure but with more texture. How rigid and generic the medical history is, how insistent its narrative arc which demands a patient's experience must always have a forward thrust, smelted by a doctor's interrogation, examination and investigations towards the shiny target of diagnosis and treatment. Without being led, Lisa's instinct is to convey her experience quite differently, with less shape and momentum. And in her own version, what comes across isn't a clear sense of progress, but a feeling of being trapped in a never-ending cycle of medical details and interactions which may describe but don't resolve her disease. This machine is my life, she tells me, dialysis is my life. And I see suddenly that the dimension in which a person with chronic disease lives differently than a healthy one isn't just space, but time.

Aristotle said time is universal, an independent dimension that exists whether we perceive it or not. Isaac Newton agreed that time is an objective reality, one which we structure into units. These views fit intuitively not just with common sense, but also the model of calendar and clock time which runs Western modern healthcare.

In the early twentieth century, philosophers lost their monopoly on this subject. Scientists started to engage with it as well and their new perspective soon undermined all that was previously thought certain. The Big Bang theory asserted that time isn't a constant that exists outside of our experience, since it began at the same moment as the universe, about 13.8 billion years ago. And Albert Einstein revolutionised the way we look at this fundamental dimension by proving with his General Theory of Relativity that, far from being universal, time is affected by gravity and acceleration, differing measurably between things, depending on their frame of reference. There are as many timelines as there are objects, he declared. Two identical, synchronised clocks put on top of Everest and at sea level will diverge by about thirty microseconds per year. These time-dilation effects influence all clocks, even biological ones like our organs.

But the philosophy of time that makes most sense to me is phenomenology. Distinguishing between objective and subjective time, phenomenologists note that we humans perceive the two quite differently. No wonder it's hard to get to grips with the mindfulness programme, with its exhortation to live in the now. According to these thinkers, time can't be separated out into pure units. Our present is always imbued with the past as well as being spiced with a sort of protention into the future. Martin Heidegger famously formulated life as being-in-time which is always a form of being-towards-death. Edmund Husserl distinguished between the objective time of clocks and subjective time, which is the stream of consciousness in which we experience duration and temporality.

Jean-Paul Sartre was probably the first to explore how a phenomenological engagement with time might elucidate aspects of disease, and specifically pain. But two modern thinkers – importantly, both also patients – have taken this to the next level. Havi Carel, a brilliant philosopher who suffers from chronic lung disease, explains it like this: 'The world of the ill is different in many ways to the world of the healthy. Its space and time are different.' S. Kay Toombs, who

lives with multiple sclerosis, adds that while the objective dimension of clock time is the one doctors are
expected to work by, its rhythm is completely out of
sync with the altogether more subjective time signa-
ture of a patient's illness. If we could only tackle the
'incommensurability' between these two time zones,
Toombs argues, we would solve many problems of
doctor–patient communication.

Friday. I wake to the sound of the waves and the comforting hum of the central heating coming on. I've slept
well. I pee to release my kidneys' overnight work. I sit
with a cup of tea in bed – enough to take up two thirds
of Lisa's daily fluid quota – looking at a sea that has
even rollers coming in one after another, just catching
the beginning of the sunlight, each wave rising like a
stripe of darkness before folding in on itself. Outside
the coldness pricks at my nostrils. The grass is rimed
with frost, the roads striped silver. Habit leads me
through a crystal drive of branches and sky and fields.
When I get there, the car park is empty and the tarmac
glinting. Lisa is in a different bed. She must have been
in all of them hundreds of times.

 Our chat meanders. She tells me she used to work
in a bank. How she tried to end her life in her early

twenties by drinking antifreeze, wrecking her kidneys, and is still paying for the event twenty years later. I know I'm not going to live a long life, she says. Five to ten years is about average on dialysis, though some get a few extra. She's more aware of time and how precious it is than before, but it's complicated. You can't do much with a needle sticking out of your arm, just read or watch TV, so the hours pass slowly. Two days off over the weekend are all very well but, by Sunday, she doesn't feel so good anymore.

It's in the news every day now: the NHS is more stretched than ever. Backlogs in surgery, cancer treatment and GP appointments have reached record levels in the UK, with 7 million people waiting to be seen. We shouldn't wonder that our failing system responds in the only way it can, by squeezing resources, the most precious of which are minutes and hours. But it's foolish to imagine there won't be serious human consequences. Because time isn't just an economic unit. It isn't some inert filing system into which tasks can simply be squeezed. It is a profound philosophical dimension in which other vital things do or don't take place: creativity, invention, connection, care. The fact these things are hard to commodify shouldn't blind us to their importance. An overextended nurse has no hope of offering succour. A time-strapped doctor can barely be expected to make a diagnosis, let alone turn away from the computer long enough to look their patient in the eye.

I've seen that time is experienced radically differently by the well and the chronically ill. While my own kidneys do their silent duty 168 hours a week without fanfare, Lisa must navigate not just the twelve hours she spends in dialysis, but the many more she is either travelling to or from it, preparing or recovering. While I sit next to her humming machine, hatching plans for the rest of my day, here one week gone the next, her past and future collapse into a present that is all about the demands of her condition.

But freedom in time is about much more than the ability to arrange one's own schedule without constraint. It's the liberty to move within and shape our own stories. Sitting at Lisa's bedside on my last morning at Greenview, I'm aware of the point when my attention starts to tip from this place back towards my own life. Not so far away, my family are waiting. The Christmas tree is in its net, ready to be released so its branches bounce down. It's time for the familiar happy routines of my life to resume. And yet, when I walk out of the dialysis centre, I could swear that – just briefly – the whole world pauses, the very leaves in the trees becoming still, the waves in the distance freezing with the spray lifting off their backs . . . before they curl to make new waves, and the moment turns into a new moment, each second bearing me towards a future nothing could have prepared me for.

From: GWeston@hotmail.com
To: heartsurgeon@lhc.nhs.com
Subject: mitral valve repair
Date: 21 February 2024

Dear Mr S,

Thanks for being at the MDT meeting a couple of
weeks ago.

I know it's not my area. But all the academic papers
I've read suggest the heart's best chance of recovering
from MR is with early intervention. If an operation is
inevitable, and given I accept the risks, there must be
clear advantages to acting sooner rather than later?

I'd be very grateful for some clarity on when you might be
happy to operate on my valve.

Gratefully as always,
Gabriel

From: heartsurgeon@lhc.nhs.co.uk
To: GWeston@hotmail.com
Subject: Re: mitral valve repair
Date: 27 February 2024

Hi Gabriel,

I totally understand your point of view and anxiety.
However, your mitral regurgitation hasn't yet reached
threshold and that really dictates our strategy. The papers
showing the benefit of early surgical intervention are all
in patients with <u>severe</u> mitral regurgitation.

Remember that surgery is not zero-risk. It carries a
0.5–1.0% mortality, 1% stroke risk.

Supposing I operate on you tomorrow, and you either
don't survive or have a massive disabling stroke. How
will we look back on the decision to operate? We'll think
it was a silly decision I suspect. We've taken a young
woman in her prime and ruined her life, and that of
her family.

That's why we don't operate too early. Plus, managing moderate MR without surgery is safe and has no long-term detrimental outcomes.

I agree with six-monthly echoes.

Hope this all makes sense to you. Do let me know if I can answer anything else.

HS

Brain

Did I think being a doctor would protect me? Did I imagine something going wrong with my own body was the worst that could happen? How can I describe this, the crease around which my life is folded? Forgive me the refuge of science while I try.

The cerebrum is the largest part of the brain and is split into two hemispheres, connected internally by the corpus callosum. The left hemisphere controls the right side of the body and is involved in tasks of logic, science, maths and language, whereas the right hemisphere controls the left side and is concerned with creative and artistic functions. The coiled outer layer, with its snaking sulci and deep gyri, is named the cortex or grey matter, and the white matter is situated underneath.

Both hemispheres have frontal, temporal, parietal and occipital lobes, and they do different things. The frontal lobe is where personality, emotion and judgement reside. It also generates speech from Broca's area and movement in the motor strip. The parietal lobe processes spatial sense, as well as touch, pain and temperature in its sensory strip. The temporal lobe, which sits above the ear, deals with hearing in the auditory cortex and contains Wernicke's area, essential for the interpretation of language. It's also important to how we experience emotion and memory. The occipital lobe is at the back of the cerebrum. It houses the visual cortex which allows us to see, and assign meaning to, our visual perceptions.

The cerebellum, meaning little brain, sits behind the cerebrum and is in charge of coordinating our movements and balance. The brainstem is the oldest part of the organ in evolutionary terms and connects the brain with the spinal cord underneath. It regulates functions like breathing, blood pressure and temperature, and we rely on it to stay alive.

A headache is all there is at first. It's manageable mostly, but sometimes really painful. Like on standing: one two three bang. Or on sitting up from lying down. It's ten days or so before I begin to worry. And even then, it takes a change to wake me up. First day of the school holidays and it's cut-glass perfect outside. And yet he's still in bed at lunchtime, room ablaze with sunshine, skateboard accusing him from the carpet, no phone in hand. Get out of bed, I think. Get up or there's something really wrong.

Locked away in the bony box of the skull and completely inert to the naked eye, ancient scholars could only guess at what the brain was for. The Egyptians didn't even think the organ mattered enough to preserve, sucking it out through the nose and dumping it before mummification. Aristotle believed the heart was where thinking occurred, the brain just a cold sponge for absorbing its heat. By the time of the Roman Empire, consensus had changed but, even then, lack of access restricted opinion. Galen, writing in the second century, speculated that cognition took place in the fluid-filled ventricles. And even many generations later, the drawings of Leonardo da Vinci and René Descartes betray a very limited understanding of neuroanatomy.

A breakthrough came in the mid seventeenth century when many European universities introduced public autopsies. You can see the difference between the drawings of Vesalius a century earlier, when opportunities for dissection were limited and contemporary conventions confined scientists to observing the brain sitting in its cap of skull, to this new era in which Thomas Willis was able to prise the brain from its vault. Suddenly, it was possible to reveal the intricate mechanics underneath, including the elaborate network of arteries known to this day as the Circle of Willis. *Cerebri Anatome*, published by Willis in 1664, with beautiful etchings by Christopher Wren, presented a rich new landscape of neuroanatomy that no one had previously even imagined.

I love thinking of Willis and Wren huddled together in the morgue turning conjecture into fact. Willis emptying the crania of dead people, pausing briefly to honour the precious moment when the brain seems to hang in the balance between being the organ of self and the object of pure science. Wren sitting somewhere nearby with his drawing board, itching to commit his impressions to paper. Were they friends? Did they go out drinking afterwards and ponder the singular metaphysical strangeness of this endeavour, their manly brains exercised in mapping the brains of others, trying with knife and pen to inch closer to the truth of what makes us human? Did they marvel at how closely the brain holds its secrets?

Feel around the geography of the new danger. Find an escape route. Leave the Emergency Department and walk out under the wide winter sky. Cram rotten words back into the consultant's grey face. Blank his prim mouthing of cancer. Crash the CT scanner to unknot that four-centimetre cerebellar mass. Loosen its pixels out of their tight, stippled constellation. Turn your attention anywhere else. Amygdala: the danger centre, an almond-shaped set of neurons deep in the medial temporal lobe, primed by the receipt of terrifying information from eyes and ears. On red alert now, firing off to the hypothalamus, in its dark recess of skull. Giving your body just one choice. Flee. Or get ready for the fight of your life.

If you hold a brain in your hands, it looks solid and inscrutable, but it's really the organ of ultimate flux, information shooting like stars from one hemisphere to the other, between lobes, from one gyrus to the next and across trillions of synapses too tiny for even the microscope to see. All of this is made possible by a rich blood supply. Internal carotid arteries bring blood to the front of the brain. The basilar artery supplies the back, and the two systems form a circuit that goes round and round. Venous blood collects in deep grooves called sinuses and these all drain to the internal jugular veins, and down to the heart.

The operational unit of the brain is the neuron. One tenth the diameter of a human hair, each of these consists of a cell body, dendrites and an axon.

Dendrites branch out, like fronds of seaweed, and receive electrical messages from hundreds of other neurons. These travel to the cell body, which contains genetic material in its nucleus, where a decision is made about whether a signal should travel onwards. Outgoing electrical messages are conducted down the axon to its tip, where little sacs open and empty neurotransmitters into the synapse, the space between one neuron and another. These chemicals are taken up by receptors on the dendrites of the receiving neuron. And so the process continues.

We've only known about this basic aspect of brain physiology for about a hundred years, and its discovery earned an Italian called Camillo Golgi and a Spaniard called Santiago Cajal the 1906 Nobel Prize. Before them, scientists had been baffled by their attempts to characterise brain tissue by looking down the microscope. They couldn't make head or tail of its indecipherable tangled meshwork. But, in 1873, Golgi developed a new staining technique that highlighted only a portion of the brain's substance. As if shading his eyes from the dazzling sun, not seeing so much enabled Golgi to focus on what was actually there.

It took Cajal to complete the loop. Despite artistic ambitions, this young Spaniard had been persuaded to go to medical school by his father. Using Golgi's staining technique, Cajal embarked on a monumental project, drawing over 3,000 intricate pictures of the varied microscopic landscape of different regions of the brain. He may have begun by scratching a creative itch, but Cajal ended up making a crucial scientific discovery, that the brain is made of a range of individual nerve cells which talk to each other.

Thinking about how the brain works is like looking up at the night sky. People respond to its vastness differently. Cajal said realising that everything communicates with everything else is 'equivalent to declaring the absolute unsearchability of the organ of the soul'. Neurobiologist Steve Rose marvels with statistics: cut out 50 mm^3 of brain and you have, in this one sample, 5 million neurons, 50 billion synapses, 22 kilometres of dendrites and 220 kilometres of axons. But Emily Dickinson puts it best. The brain is 'wider than the sky', 'deeper than the sea', and 'just the weight of God'.

Dexamethasone for swelling. Blue light across town to where the sick kids go. Wheelchair down corridors, up lift and home to a ward with a cuddly name and no stinting on Christmas decorations. Straight to bed, legs curled up, too tall for the colourful cot. A welcome tour: our very own fridge, the coffee room and shower, a quick lesson in how to fold the armchair down to make a bed. But don't sit just yet. Come now and meet him. Serene neurosurgeon, sleeves rolled up against infinite work. The room is tight with no good news. Won't see his next birthday, whisper the walls. The monitor flickers. I'll get out what I can, he says. But first I need more scans.

Sometimes, it takes an illness to show us how things are. Epilepsy has done more to integrate the textured detail of individual human experience with anatomy than anything else in the history of neuroscience. Epilepsy occurs when a transient abnormal electrical discharge in the brain results in a seizure. This may involve a large part of the brain, or as few as 2,000 neurons. The symptoms associated with a seizure exactly reflect the normal function of the involved brain. For example, a fit occurring in Broca's area in the frontal lobe would interfere with a patient's ability to talk.

Seizure symptoms are as complex as the brain that gives rise to them, and this has enabled genera- tions of neurologists to harness epilepsy as a tool for assembling intricate maps of brain function. In 1909, the German anatomist Korbinian Brodmann split the cortex into fifty-two areas by the cell microarchitec- ture that had fascinated Cajal, and neurologists still use his scheme for identifying the location of seizures.

Hans Berger recorded the first electroencephalogram (EEG) in 1924, dotting multiple electrodes across the scalp and measuring both the regular brainwaves of normal synaptic transmission, and the abnormal spikes of electrical instability that come with epilepsy. EEG is often combined these days with video telemetry: a patient is observed in a clinical room, for days to weeks and, as seizures occur, they are recorded by video and EEG, enabling a precise correlation between brain activity and human experience. It's hard to believe that Berger was so consumed by self-doubt that he didn't publish his discovery of EEG for five years. He would have been amazed to know how relevant it still is, a century on.

Neurosurgeon Wilder Penfield showed no such tentativeness. He pioneered the Montreal Procedure in the 1930s, an operation for isolating and ablating clusters of brain cells responsible for his patients' fits, while they lay awake under his knife. Noting they felt no discomfort, he took the opportunity to stimulate healthy areas of his patients' brains after completing their surgery, while carefully observing their reactions. This meticulous work of neurostimulation generated Penfield's homunculus, an idiosyncratic cartoon depicting a man languishing across a brain, each part of his body touching the section of cortex in which the corresponding motor or sensory processing takes place.

Epilepsy medicine remains at the forefront of brain exploration. At Queen Square in London, the National Hospital for Neurology and Neurosurgery, a trial to assess a new tool called stereo-encephalography is underway. Multiple long electrodes are inserted through the skull and deep into the brain to record seizure activity. The hope is that this precision mapping will facilitate previously unthinkable surgery in the one third of epilepsy patients whose focal seizures are still not treatable with medicines. Maybe we'll soon be using tiny probes to analyse normal brain tissue, furnishing scientists with unimaginably rich 3-D maps of neuronal activity. When you look at the history of neuroscience, it's clear that investigating the brain has never been about confirming knowledge we already have. With new ways of looking, come totally unexpected revelations.

Cars and lorries crash upside down on the wall, the movie projected topsy-turvy next to the MRI so he can view it in the mirror by his eyes while being scanned. Sitting alongside the machine, the noise is deafening, its regular rhythmic sound arranging itself into jibes in my head so that I have to replace my ear defenders. A blaring din, then sixty minutes of cracking, thumping and sirens. The huge, grey bulk has swallowed him whole. He is like a magician's assistant, only hair and feet poking out. The scanner bangs again and the whole bed shakes. His eye finds mine in the lipstick-small mirror. He holds my gaze awhile, before returning to *Fast and Furious*, the movie's picture glitching from the magnet.

What the machine knows. New patient in my maw. Still and quiet, his face mask down. Liquid helium swishes round to cool the superconducting magnet from my last charge. A human is seventy per cent water. Each water molecule contains two hydrogen atoms. That's billions across the body. In the middle of each hydrogen atom is a proton, spinning on its axis, a tiny little compass. Out in the world, the protons inside a person are randomly orientated but look what happens now. I turn on the full 1.5 tesla of my magnet – powerful enough to pluck a car from the ground – and the protons inside all this boy's hydrogen atoms line up like soldiers. Then I apply a gradient of radio frequency to knock the orderly protons out of alignment. When I switch it off again, the protons bounce back. No wonder it's noisy. I measure the signal the protons emit as they realign, map each tiny voxel of tissue with little cameras. Assemble the beautiful data into a picture.

The neurosurgeon comes to find me on the ward. We go into the corridor and sit by the computer. For comparison, he shows me yesterday's CT. I angle my face to the screen but blur my eyes. I don't want to see it anymore. Then he clicks on the MRI. I prepare myself to hear that my son's spine is as full of tumour as his brain.

The surgeon flicks through images, axial and coronal sections. He credits me with more medical know-how than I am capable of. This ventricle, that lobe, this vessel, all the details collapse before my eyes. But then he stops on one picture and something inside me wakes up. The mass appears different here. It's clean-looking, cartoon-bright. He has to repeat himself several times, before I hear what he's explaining to me. Cancer doesn't have this appearance on an MRI. This isn't a tumour, it's blood.

It's taken centuries to get a decent view of the brain. Wilhelm Röntgen demonstrated the first X-ray in 1895. But his discovery wasn't very useful for examining an organ whose soft tissue constitution renders it nearly invisible to this spectrum. In 1918, Walter Dandy produced great pictures with ventriculography, a technique that meant draining cerebrospinal fluid from ventricles and replacing it with air. But the procedure caused hazardous changes to patients' intracranial pressure, so it didn't last. 1927 saw the first cerebral arteriogram and then, in the 1970s, the landscape of neuroimaging was transformed by William Oldendorf and Godfrey Hounsfield's discovery of CT scans. After generations of gloom, these density maps, which build a picture of the organ based on differential absorption of X-rays, felt as magical as taking photographs from inside the skull.

The arrival of MRI in the 1980s went a step further. With none of the dangerous radiation of CT scans, this new technology provided unparalleled clarity in looking at the anatomy and pathology of the brain. In its wake came other more dynamic ways of scrutinising cerebral activity moment to moment. Franciscus Donders had used mental chronometry in 1868 to measure reaction times during simple cognitive tasks. Angelo Mosso had attempted a rudimentary measurement of the redistribution of blood during emotional and intellectual activity a couple of years later. But now, by applying statistical analysis comparing blood flow at rest and during mental activity, functional MRI was able to pinpoint the areas of the brain being used for a particular purpose to within a few millimetres. fMRI has led to the invention of all sorts of other scans, SPECT and PET to name just a couple, which each have specific utility in assessing brain diseases like Alzheimer's and Parkinson's.

There are real limitations to neuroimaging. On the funny side, a 2009 study on a dead salmon showed false signals that looked like brain activity when the fish was tested with fMRI, a salutary reminder that we should interpret all data with caution. More seriously, some types of disease seem to have been sidelined rather than assisted by the burgeoning field of neuroimaging. Though neurological disorders are depicted with ever increasing accuracy, psychiatric ones are harder to capture. And this inevitably leads to bias, the patient with a brain tumour or encephalitis given a type of medical credence, while the one with mental illness comes to seem less important, just because we don't yet know how to identify their pathology with scans. Perhaps most scary, though, is that the sheer availability of modern imaging can lead to cockiness. We may be so seduced by the sophistication of our pictures that we forget to look at our patients.

They say we're safe to go home. We bring the Christmas tree in from the garden where we left it, still in its corset of netting. The hospital leaflets lie next to the box of fairy lights. Cavernomas are abnormal clusters of blood vessels, one tells me. I put the tinsel on. They occur in the brains of one in 600 in the population, but only cause symptoms in one in 400,000. I hang the papier mâché decorations the kids made when they were small. Seizures and brain haemorrhage are the two most serious consequences. These cavernomas present surgeons with a perilous dilemma: is it riskier to take them out or leave them alone?

On Christmas Day, the whole family congratulates him. Of course, he's too tired to sit up at the table with the rest of us, no wonder opening presents doesn't appeal. The lights flicker on the tree. I tell myself he's happy lying there with my choice of carols from Cambridge. Days go by and we dole out oral steroids. I make him walk to the bottom of the garden because I want him to regain balance. I throw a lemon into his shaking left hand and make him move clothes pegs along pieces of cardboard. I wedge a pen into his grip and put it back there when he drops it.

Before New Year, I wake to find the house yellow with lights on in the middle of the night. He is vomiting. At the hospital an hour later, they tell us he's bleeding again. They hurry the scans across London to the neurosurgeons who reply that it's not bad enough to require immediate intervention so, after a day of observation, we return home. It's different now. He lies on his left side on the sofa. He doesn't complain.

He can't turn over and isn't able to get up without one of us supporting him. That night, foxes scream in the gloaming as I try to divine the vascular events playing out in his brain. The next morning, he says he feels like his body's not working anymore and I suddenly know with complete clarity that we are running out of time.

In some ways, it feels like we have moved mountains. Neurological treatments have surpassed all expectation. Focused ultrasound is targeting lesions deep in the brain without damaging surrounding tissue. Patients with paralysis are being helped to move again. Retinal implants are reversing blindness. And we are developing new investigations all the time too. We now use pulsed laser illumination to examine synapse action in real time. We can combine genetics and imaging to look at interactions, not just between individual neurons, but among the ions and proteins inside them. Huge advances are being made with stem cell research and brain–computer interfaces. A whole mouse connectome has been delineated, its brain cut into 10,000 slices each less than thirty nanometres thick, then scanned by an electron microscope and reconstructed in glorious Technicolor.

But brain surgery is still just surgery. However hifa-lutin neuroscience becomes, however precocious our advances, we each have only one brain, that selfsame solid organ that Aristotle and Thomas Willis pored over centuries ago, resting in its container of bone. Reassuringly physical. Frighteningly simple. This is a soft organ inside a tight box. If you have an injury and it swells up too much, you die.

A porter arrives with a stretcher and my son says no. The porter offers to get a wheelchair and he declines again. He rises slowly from the bed, head as stiff as a doll's. He moves unsteadily, with a nurse on one side and the pair of us on the other, all the way to the lift. He stands and waits until it arrives, and holds himself up inside it, and walks out and all the way down the corridor to the anaesthetic room. I am leading him to his fate, to a place where his scalp and skull and brain will be cut open. And God knows what will happen next. I concentrate instead on the sound of the lift door, the floor's gleam, the cream walls that mark where the ordinary corridor becomes the surgical corridor. I rest my gaze on the competent face of the woman anaesthetist. He lies down and I take his hand. We look at each other while he counts slowly, getting much further than expected, and I keep my own face steady until the moment when he lets go.

When the American artist William Utermohlen was diagnosed with Alzheimer's, he decided to chart the course of his illness with a series of self-portraits, one completed every year until his death in 2007. This little chronicle is the opposite of the history of neuroscience, the capacity for seeing and the available information dwindling with each of the eight pictures. Utermohlen's self-portraits bear sequential witness to the absolute disintegration of one man's identity and illustrate how, when the brain is damaged, it slips from its logical anchor, fragmenting reality. But not all brain diseases end badly.

I stand at the top of the driveway and watch him getting smaller. In the quiet morning, the only sound is the roar of wheels on tarmac. He's thinner than he was a month ago, and I am too. He's a bit shaky on his skateboard, as I feel shaky in my heart. His hood is up, concealing what lies underneath, a soft white dressing and below that a narrow shaved strip and five-inch wound, black with blood and stitches. As for me? I am changed in every cell of my body. I think of all that I've learned from books about the brain and the things I've seen in the past few weeks that I never thought I'd see. And I bring my scattered mind to stillness on one point, which is the brain's limitless capacity for fresh knowledge, for repair, for life. In the distance, he attempts the tiniest of jumps, feet barely breaking contact with the board. And for the first time, I dare to imagine he'll soon be up to his old tricks again.

Liver

How do I begin again?

I stand for a moment, waiting for my heart to settle, then walk through the porticoed main entrance.

I've come to see heroic surgery. Living donation liver transplant involves a healthy person giving part of this organ to someone who's sick, usually a relative. Fewer than one in ten liver transplants in the UK are living donations, the operation performed at just three hospitals where the best specialists are. This is because it's risky. We have only one liver, so there's no room for error. The surgeon has to strike a perfect balance, harvesting the right amount of tissue for the sick recipient, while leaving enough for the donor to survive.

Inside, the hospital is as familiar as a childhood home. The smell is like the smell of self.

The transplant coordinator appears, and we head straight down the corridor. Today's patient is a five-year-old suffering from a rare genetic disorder, she says. Normally, a chain of liver-cell reactions enables nitrogen to be turned into urea, which gets eliminated by the kidneys. But if a key hepatic enzyme is missing, urea can't be converted and accumulates dangerously in the blood as ammonia. Without treatment, brain damage occurs. The disease can be slowed with drugs and a low-protein diet, but transplant offers the only cure.

At the paeds ward, she stops, saying she'll meet me there. So I carry on, and am soon pushing through the double doors that lead to main theatres. It was here I rushed as an insatiable junior, eager to spend any spare moment assisting, here I became shiny-drenched for the first time when a patient bled out, where I sweated through my virgin solo appendicectomy. I pass the empty reception desk and remember the senior sister who would sit barking friendly recriminations at us all, how bulletproof I used to feel. In the changing room, I shrug on a scrub top and bottom, before resting on the slatted wooden bench.

Upstairs, adjoining theatres are being set up for synchronous surgery. I pause at the door, as the father lies down on the operating table, confirming his name and date of birth. And when the anaesthetist asks him to count to ten, I momentarily see my son's face as he counted towards an unconsciousness I wasn't sure he'd wake from.

But then the patient's eyes close and I step into the room, and the simple surgical mechanics I have loved all my life start to take over. Quiet turns to hubbub. A nurse inserts a catheter, and a radio flares into song. The liver reg shaves and preps the abdomen, brown-daubing it, unfurling drapes to frame a precise square of nakedness with green. The perfusionist sets up the cell-saver, a machine no liver transplant can begin without, whose job it is to collect, wash and quickly reinfuse blood lost during surgery if such losses prove to be massive. The transplant coordinator writes the name of the operation on the whiteboard: left lateral segment resection for living donation. When they refer to him now, he is the donor, not the father, not even the patient, and I'm just thinking how key these clinical semiotics are to a surgeon's ability to function when the consultant steps up to the table. With one deft movement, the donor abdomen opens under his knife like an eye. He penetrates the peritoneum, revealing a landscape of pristine abdominal anatomy. And there, at the centre of the surgical field, is the liver.

The liver is the largest solid organ in the body. Held snugly in place by the diaphragm, this dense pyramid of tissue occupies the entire right upper abdomen, and some of the left too. Deceptively plain from the front, its smooth maroon surface broken only by a swirl of peritoneum called the falciform ligament, the back of the liver tells a different story. Here, a cluster of anatomical structures points to just how industrious it is. That navy-blue vessel, thicker than your thumb, is the inferior vena cava, which carries all the blood from the liver and lower body to the heart. This bright green structure, the size and colour of a partly deflated birthday balloon, is the gallbladder, where bile gets stored. And that complicated looking hub is the porta hepatis, through which most of the liver's main vessels pass in and out.

What does the liver do? Famously, detoxification. Like a giant filter, it sifts blood arriving from the gut in the hepatic portal vein, gobbling up bacteria, fungi, parasites and cellular debris. It breaks down old red blood cells. It converts ammonia to urea, and produces enzymes which turn hormones, drugs and alcohol into harmless metabolites. It's also a nutritional mecca. Glucose not needed straightaway is converted into glycogen, for quick release between meals when sugar levels drop. Fatty acids morph into a form of energy called adenosine triphosphate. And amino acids are topped up for building proteins. But the liver isn't just a waste disposal unit-cum-larder. It makes stuff too. Bile – which helps digest fat and carries away detritus from the blood – is created here, as are cholesterol and albumin, clotting and immune factors, and the hormones we need for regulating sexual function. A helpful bonus from all this activity is heat. The liver is so busy that the energy it generates warms the blood that courses through it.

It's hard to do justice in a few lines to an organ with more than 500 vital functions to its name. But I'm happy to confess as much, keep my paean brief and turn the spotlight elsewhere. Because what really grips me about the liver isn't its standard physiology, the virtuoso performance it pulls off in fairweather conditions, but the unique way this organ is able to respond to danger.

The surgeon strokes the silky liver with his finger, trying to establish where, below its treacherous and gleaming surface, the main vessels divide into their constituent branches. If he misjudges the next step, there will be catastrophic bleeding. I think of what the neurosurgeon told me after my son's operation, that the blood in his brain was under great pressure when they cut him open, forgetting in his own post-op relief, that I would be listening as a mother not a doctor. He leans against me – I feel the heat and weight of him – as he mobilises the left lateral segment, a quarter of the organ's overall volume and a perfect fit for this father's child. He identifies the porta hepatis, burrowing deeper to isolate the tributaries he needs to preserve if the graft is to survive. His hands are steady, but I can hear him muttering as he searches for the portal vein. I can smell it, but I can't see it. Steady now, steady.

Then he is scooping the lump of flesh up in both hands and placing it in the shiny bowl the scrub nurse holds out to him. He looks at me over his glasses and nods, a tacit cue for me to follow her next door, to where the beautiful denouement of this surgical scene is about to unfold, the thing I've surely come to see. Where, within a landscape of green, a boy's abdomen lies open like a book, his miniature organs shining like jewels. Where a second transplant surgeon is waiting, small hands crossed over her chest, ready to reach in and remove the tiny liver she has separated from its mooring, spent after just five years of life. Soon, I will stand there, witnessing how she lowers the father's life-saving segment into his son's body and watching – with the admiration only a person who has tried and failed to reach such a level of expertise can know – how she crafts each delicate anastomosis, to supply fresh blood to this transplanted liver and bring it back to life. But right now, I can't move. I am rooted to the spot, staring into the deep, dark hole of the father's abdomen, at the singed and tatty edge of his cut organ, asking myself one question. How – after an injury as great as this – is it possible for a person to repair themselves?

In 1931, scientists G. M. Higgins and R. M. Anderson performed a groundbreaking experiment. Keen to test the liver's mythologised capacity for regeneration, they threw caution to the wind, anaesthetised a rat, and summarily chopped out two thirds of this part of its body. What happened next amazed them. Not only did the rodent survive – an assault of this magnitude to any other vital organ would almost certainly have proved fatal – but its recovery looked more like magic than medicine. Hunched over the rat's splayed abdomen, hands still wet from surgery, the two men could swear the tissue was starting to regrow in front of their eyes. Three days later, there was no doubt. The liver had returned entirely to its original size and function.

Living donation liver surgery, pioneered in Chicago in 1989 and introduced to this country seven years later, would never have been possible without this first experiment. But it's the countless subsequent partial hepatectomies that have enabled scientists not just to witness the apparent miracle of liver regeneration for themselves, but to start understanding how it works. The first surprise is the fact that tissue renewal in this organ isn't performed by stem cells, as is usually the case in places of high turnover, such as the skin or gut. Here, the microscopic powerhouse is a cell called the hepatocyte, which accounts for more than eighty per cent of the organ's mass. Let's get our bearings.

A liver has two main lobes. Both are divisible into eight segments, each of which contains 1,000 lobules measuring one millimetre in diameter. It's easy to picture these collectively, a grid of perfectly symmetrical hexagonal units, slotted into each other like cells in a beehive. But I want to get us nearer to the action. See how this individual lobule has a central vein and six sentry-posts at its outer angles? Known as portal triads, these microscopic replicas of the porta hepatis all contain a tiny branch of the hepatic artery, portal vein and bile duct. Bile drains outwards towards the portal triads, while blood flows inwards towards the central vein, along wispy vessels called sinusoids. Perforations in the sinusoid walls allow blood to pass into a zone called the Space of Disse. And this is where all the hepatocytes are, ready to perform not only the liver's metabolic work, but its grand trick of regeneration too.

Unlike most other cells, hepatocytes are frequently blessed with more than one nucleus, and it's the extra synthetic power provided by this doubling of their

DNA that equips them to respond so well to injury. When a piece of liver is cut out, over a hundred extra genes get expressed, triggering a cascade of chemical reactions which stimulate the remaining hepatocytes to repopulate, which they do by swelling first in size and then in number. The cell biology may be hard to grasp, but the liver's versatility never ceases to wow me. A big dog's liver, transplanted into a small dog, will shrink until it perfectly fits the abdomen of the recipient. Fragments of liver, transplanted to remote sites around the body, will start to grow at the same time as the mother organ if partial hepatectomy takes place. The ancient story of Prometheus, his eagle-pecked liver doomed to heal daily for all eternity, may be pushing it, but not by much. A single liver really can grow back after as many as twelve consecutive partial resections.

Of course, all this begs an obvious question. If the liver is so good at regenerating, why does anyone get liver failure in the first place, or end up needing a transplant? The simple answer is that hepatocytes don't respond in quite the same way to disease as they do to surgery. But before I can elaborate, here are a few background facts.

Mortality from liver disease has soared by 400 per cent in the last fifty years. There are more than a hundred genetic, autoimmune and vascular conditions that can plague this organ, but the truth is that ninety per cent of liver disease is caused by just three things: viral hepatitis, fatty liver and alcohol.

The dangers of alcohol are well publicised, and many are aware of hepatitis B and C, viral infections which are usually transmitted by blood or other bodily fluids. But the most aggressive new threat on the scene, non-alcoholic liver disease, is still relatively unheard of. The British Liver Trust estimates that one in three adults in the UK have early signs of this condition, and predict that its serious form, non-alcoholic steatohepatitis – or NASH – will become the commonest cause of cirrhosis and end-stage liver failure in the UK over the next decade. You'd be right to assume the obese are most vulnerable. But recent research indicates that a high-sugar diet is enough to put someone at risk even if they don't consume much fat. Non-alcoholic fatty liver disease has been found both in children and those of normal weight.

Here's the thing though. When it comes to liver disease, it doesn't much matter what the cause is, the pathological sequence is the same. First comes inflammation. If the trigger persists, this turns into a stiffening of the organ, called fibrosis. And if there is still no relief, cirrhosis – characterised by scarring, abnormal nodules and vascular changes – sets in. Hepatocytes fare very well against the first two of these – regeneration, like forgiveness, can happen so many times a person takes it for granted. But when liver failure occurs, there is no turning back. Sometimes this can be quite sudden. Fulminant hepatic failure occurs in previously well people when their liver suffers a sudden and massive injury such as a viral infection, paracetamol overdose, or deathcap mushroom poisoning.

More common are those with chronic liver disease, which has progressed beyond the early, reversible stages to cirrhosis. This marks the point where the organ has given up the ghost and can no longer repair itself. As well as jaundice and confusion, cirrhotic patients are often thin but with fluid-bloated abdomens and ankles, and may arrive at hospital bleeding from the mouth or anus. For the individual in this situation, the options are stark. They either get a liver transplant or they die.

It's Friday lunchtime and a queue is forming outside the large conference room. Some come from the direction of the canteen, sandwich or coffee in hand. Everyone pauses to take a list from the pile by the door. By the time I'm inside, most of the seats around the oval table are already full. The professor who's been my host this week smiles, before turning back to the transplant surgeon who performed the first part of the living donation. An anaesthetist in scrubs leans across the table, to chat with a couple of Intensive Therapy Unit (ITU) consultants. The familiar taxonomy of NHS uniforms helps me identify an occupational therapist and a couple of physios, some nurses – one of whom wears a badge that says 'alcohol specialist' – and a social worker. The hepatologist, whose ward rounds I've been tagging along with, stands at the front of the room, sleeves rolled up, talking on his mobile phone. A junior doctor sets up her laptop on the table, the gleam of too much work on her skin and hair. I squeeze in beside someone on the windowsill, and remind myself of the facts as the weekly Transplant List meeting looks set to begin.

1,000 liver transplant operations are performed every year in the UK. 500 people are waiting for one right now and fifteen per cent of them will die before this happens. There are seven transplant centres, each with its own list, and a patient can be on only one. This hospital – the biggest centre in Europe, performing more than a fifth of the nation's liver transplants – currently has 200 hopefuls on its books, from as far away as Belfast, Plymouth, Bristol and Derriford.

A prized place on the transplant list is granted by nationally agreed criteria. The first is the UK Model for

End-stage Liver Disease (UKELD) score. This number predicts the likelihood that someone will die imminently from liver cirrhosis, and is arrived at by analysing a range of blood results which build a picture of a person's liver function and overall physiological status. A patient needs a score of at least 49, and this is reviewed every month. Having a UKELD in the right range essentially shows you're sick enough to need a transplant, while remaining sufficiently robust to survive one. But if being eligible for a liver transplant were as simple as hitting a numerical target, there would be no need for a meeting. The second determining factor, of equal weight to the UKELD, but far less quantifiable, is what gets said in this room.

The consultant steps up to the lectern, and begins introducing today's patients. For the first couple, all I glean is jargon plus verdict. Fifty-three-year-old female, Caroli's syndrome, associated with polycystic kidneys and recent biliary sepsis. UKELD 50: LIST. Or thirty-five-year-old male, childhood biliary atresia, with Kasai procedure at birth. Acutely decompensating with upper GI bleed and encephalopathy. UKELD 54: LIST.

But as the conversation expands around more nuanced scenarios, I start to tune in properly. A woman half my age, with autoimmune disease and TB, creates a quandary, because her UKELD score is one point shy of where it needs to be. The junior doctor fills in the gaps: she's currently free from ascites, encephalopathy and varices, but it won't be long. An anaesthetist briefs on her overall fitness and confirms she's up to surgery. A dietician comments that her anthropomorphics look good. A social worker vouches for her positive attitude: we didn't pull her over the line, she came. Everyone agrees this woman is sick enough for a transplant and doing all she can to get listed. The doctor chairing the meeting looks distressed. The UKELD classification is the best system there is, he says, but sometimes it doesn't properly serve the individual patient. A unanimous decision is made to take the rare step of referring her for national appeal.

Another case divides opinion. There's no doubt the patient in question is ill enough to warrant a transplant. The sticking point is whether she can survive one. The specialist alcohol nurse vouches for her abstinence, but when the physician asks how much reconditioning can be expected, the dietician replies she has no muscle mass and a low BMI. In the end, the group reaches consensus: objective parameters should be set for this woman, and her case rediscussed in a month.

The next couple of patients aren't so lucky. A sixty-year-old woman with NASH cirrhosis, who's been waiting over a year for a new liver, is promptly delisted because of a recent diagnosis of bowel cancer. A sixty-five-year-old man is deemed to have become too frail for a transplant and is also removed. Regardless of outcome, though, the week's patients are carefully presented and discussed, many in great detail, not only in terms of their liver disease and state of general physiology, but also their drug and alcohol history, mental capacity and lifestyle, and degree of family or other personal support.

I've attended multidisciplinary meetings all my working life, weekly sessions where doctors gather to exchange complex information, and the best possible plan is reached for each patient, within the context of a usually unspoken understanding that resources are limited, and not everything can be done for everyone. I am also a patient in this system. Every year, at the Royal Brompton Hospital, a doctor announces my name, presents the salient details of my cardiac history and the incremental progress of my disease, and a conversation whose necessary candour precludes my own presence, culminates in a verdict being reached about the timing of my heart surgery. But I have never witnessed a meeting like this one.

There is nothing abstract about what is happening here. Right now, in this conference room, life and death decisions are being made, the allocation of precious organs considered or denied. This is a Multidisciplinary Teams meeting like no other, where patients must balance on a knife-edge between illness and fitness to be granted even a shot at salvation; where staff who spend most of their week caring for these very patients, without moralising about how they ended up in liver failure, must shed sentiment to become judge and jury. I think of something I once heard Yo-Yo Ma say, that what made Bach such an extraordinary composer was his ability to balance compassion for humanity with a ruthless objectivity. And I suddenly realise that it's exactly this quality, the capacity for a kind of moral ambiguity, that I've witnessed on the Liver Unit and that has impressed me more deeply than anything I've seen in all my years in medicine. The doctor chairing this meeting is also the person I've studied on the wards, not just helping newly transplanted patients accept their new livers, but caring for those he's been a part of deciding won't ever get one. The surgeons whose transplant surgery I've admired are the selfsame individuals who are ready to be called out suddenly, at any hour of the day and night, to harvest organs from dead patients who, right this minute, are out in the world, living their lives, oblivious to the fact that sometime soon a completely unforeseen event will result in them dying fast and healthy enough to be in a position to donate an organ.

And perhaps it's this last observation, the reacquaintance, via this one strange and defamiliarising fact, with the sheer unpredictability of our lives, that knocks me. Because, as the last case of the meeting is presented – an HIV-positive man with a long history of alcohol and intravenous drug abuse, who has already had two liver transplants but has fallen ill again – I find I'm only half-concentrating. I'm also thinking that all the knowledge in the world can't protect us. I hear one doctor say that this guy is unreliable and resistant, someone else argue that he's managed more than six months without drinking or taking drugs, and has three small children, the prof stepping in to remind everyone that this type of liver disease is about bad biology not bad character. And though I know I'm rooting for this patient, whose wild vulnerability reminds me of some of those I love most, I'm also distracted. I consider the small canvas of sorrow of those I love. A friend is diagnosed with multiple sclerosis. A son shoots himself in a garden shed. A husband's heart is torn as he moves something in his garden. A daughter learns how to cut herself. A toddler is diagnosed with a life-shortening illness and a single mother with cancer. A sister goes to prison for an offence committed while mentally ill. A father descends into psychosis and cannot emerge. A mother succumbs to dementia. A colleague hangs himself. As the physician in charge says that time's up, and they'll need to return to this complex case next week, I look down at the list in my hand. The paper feels solid, phenomenological; I hook a fingernail under the staple at the corner, notice the grain of the paper in the sunshine, the names and ages and hospital numbers printed on the left, essential identifiers, stout and black against a background of whiteness. Sometimes, a person can't be saved by even the best medicine. So how do we begin again?

In Outpatients, sunshine carves out light-sabres of dust. Gemma is making tea for a young student who's having trouble sleeping. He tells her not a day goes by when he doesn't thank his lucky stars but, after a silence which she doesn't fill, soon admits what he really feels is angry. None of his friends have to think about their health. The pills make him tired and hungry, and give him acne. When he went back to school after his transplant a few years ago, he was bullied for being overweight, and he can't face that again. Exercising manically helps him stay in shape, but at night he feels anxious. After half an hour, a time slot the NHS would usually slot three patients into, he

leaves with a new appointment, and a sleep question-
naire. He tells Gemma he's never been able to speak as
frankly as this about his illness before.

Next door, Marianne is sitting with a sixteen-year-old
with autoimmune disease. The girl is desperate for a
new liver but not sick enough to go on the list. In the
meantime, she's been put on a tough regimen of pred-
nisolone and azathioprine, to keep her disease at bay.
The doctor remains neutral when her patient admits to
not taking her meds more than twenty per cent of the
time, and expounds on the benefits of weed, aloe vera
and turmeric. She waits for the girl to finish and asks
her what she wants to do, and I'm suddenly struck by
how much of a doctor's time is usually spent dispens-
ing wisdom, and how little accommodating a patient's
own feelings about their disease and treatment. The
more the doctor hands over control, the more the girl
starts to make eye contact and perk up and, between
them, they soon arrive at an imperfect but realistic
plan. It's a surprisingly radical thing to witness.

On Todd Ward, an engraved placard tells the caution-
ary tale of the eponymous doctor, his life abbreviated
to an ironic triad of information: commitment to liver
medicine, invention of the comforting hot toddy, and

eventual demise from alcoholic cirrhosis. In one of the cubicles, the doctor who chaired the transplant list meeting is at a patient's bedside. Continue pulsing methylprednisolone, he tells the registrar, and look for an AST of 50 or below in the next couple of days. If you don't see it, get a biopsy. Remember rejection is a histological diagnosis. When he says the word rejection, the patient pulls her dressing gown around her and starts to cry. I look away, note the bluebell print on the nylon curtains, the serosanguinous fluid coming out of the patient's drain, a card on the windowsill with love from Mum and Clive. The doctor sits down beside her. There's no need to worry, he says, taking her hand in his. The word rejection sounds awful but what we're witnessing is nothing more than the immune engagement of your new liver. This happens in half our patients and doesn't mean anything bad is happening. She nods through her tears. Get the pain team to come and review the analgesia, he asks the juniors before turning back to her. There's no rush, we'll get you home when you're good and ready.

In a side room at the end of the ward, a woman is dying. She is old but not that old, somewhere between myself and my mother. A blancmange-pink hospital nightie lies against the corrugated board of her sternum, and her arms rest on top of the clean, folded-back sheets, childlike. She was someone's child. One day, my children will be like this, when I am long gone and can't be there to comfort them. The door is slightly open and this is what I see. The doctor says the woman's name, picks up a hand from the sheets, squeezes it and then smiles – she must feel a squeeze in return. Still holding the woman's hand, she introduces herself and explains why she's here. If all I could see was the doctor, I wouldn't know she was talking to someone so far gone, it would look like she was on one end of a normal conversation. Blink if I'm making sense to you, she encourages. There is nothing so she places the hand down, but not to give up or leave. She moves around the quiet bed in the removed room and finds a sachet of artificial saliva and a small pink sponge on a little stick. She puts some on and explains what she's going to do before gently applying the sponge to the woman's lips, wetting them. There is nothing lovely about these lips. But the doctor's touch, the softness and care of it, is how someone would perform this act if these were the most voluptuous lips on earth, if this task the greatest pleasure of touch to the most beautiful mouth. So that I can believe this woman, the one on the other end of this touch, the one feeling the sponge arrive at her mouth and gently wet it with such care, would remember her own loveliness just before dying. Just imagine that, she would remember the day and the air and the smells and exactly who she was at that time, the time she cannot ever have known in the second it was happening would be the thing that provided the last lovely echo of her life.

Linda writes up three livers due for transplant today on the theatre coffee room whiteboard. The handsome Syrian surgeon, on call for transplant surgery 24/7 for the whole week, dozes with his legs slung over the arm of the short plastic sofa, dreaming about a new bicycle. In the corridor of the Institute for Liver Studies, research fellows from around the world settle at their work stations while registrars fan out to the Liver ITU and wards to check on their sickest patients before the consultants arrive. The liver pathologist clicks in the first slide from the urgent pile of biopsies that has collected over the weekend and leans into his microscope. The fifteen transplant coordinators change shifts, Agi leaving with the satisfaction of another night's work well done, but knowing it's too late to see her daughter before she's taken into theatre in a hospital across town to have her tonsillectomy. Gemma showers after her morning run, and wonders if this is the day she'll finally get round to telling everyone she's pregnant. Miriam necks the last of her coffee before going to check on her youngest post-op transplant patient. Dee and her team sit in the low light of the office, typing quietly, unaware they're the most hard-working secretaries on the planet. Posters on the walls announce the retirement of one of the two most senior professors, while his surgical coeval wheels his bicycle into the great hall of the hospital, adding another week to the three decades he's already contributed here.

I've grown wary of conclusions. But I do know this. We are not separable from those we care for, just as our strength is not separable from our vulnerability. A recent change in the law on organ donation seems to acknowledge as much, a person's willingness to help now assumed alongside their desire to be saved. Who knows, from one day to the next, what each of us might have the privilege to give or to receive.

From: GWeston@hotmail.com
To: psychmed@rbh.nhs.com
Subject: doctor/patient seeking support
Date: 25 May 2024

Dear psychology department,

I am a patient at your hospital and also an NHS doctor. I have longstanding mitral valve disease, which has progressed. I wonder if I might be eligible for an appointment with one of your team?

Kind regards,

Gabriel Weston

F87148

Heart

It's the end of the weekend and one of those autumn evenings when the air smells like gunpowder. I wheel my bike into the hall, clip lights on front and back, then return to the kitchen to check my phone. Listening out brings me a collage of sounds. There's the rhythmic thump of my son playing upstairs on the electronic drum kit and the buzz of my daughter's shower while, just next door, the twins are bickering comfortably over the PS4. We're not often together like this now, and there's a cosiness I'm reluctant to leave. But a text from one of the transplant coordinators, asking if I'd like to come and see an organ retrieval tonight, was too enticing to ignore.

My husband gets back with pizza and is calling the kids down when my phone rings. I grab a slice, jot down where I'm going and head out, without saying a proper goodbye. And maybe it's this lapse, combined with the starkness of what I know I'm going to see, that makes me look back just before I push off from the kerb, noting how just seeing my home like this – outside against inside, darkness to light – frames the ordinariness of a family weekend into a kind of wholeness that I almost can't bear to acknowledge anymore, so close did I come to losing it.

The feeling heart, the physical heart. The emotional heart versus the actual piece of muscle beating away inside each of our chests. I'm no sooner on my bike and pedalling away, the cold air filling my lungs, the throb of heat travelling from my thorax all the way down my arms and legs, than I'm making the transition I've been honing for decades in the operating theatre, turning away from what is personal and hard to fathom, towards that which can be countenanced and described and known.

Welcome back onto solid ground then. If you make a fist with your left hand and press knuckles against the reassuring solidity of your breastbone, you delineate the approximate size and position of your heart. You know the drill now, that anatomical convention is to cut an organ from its moorings, presenting it as if on the pathologist's slab. Tradition be damned! It doesn't make sense to imagine this organ still, when its defining feature is the heartbeat, a phenomenal physiological event which occurs 100,000 times a day, delivering 5,000 gallons of oxygen-rich blood to every fibre of our bodies. The heart is no inert lump of flesh, but the hub of a vast network of 60,000 miles of arteries and veins, two distinct but interconnected circuits held together in one snug embrace.

The right side of the heart is in charge of the pulmonary circulation. Veins laden with oxygen-depleted blood from around the body all converge and empty into the right atrium. This is also home to the sinoatrial node, which generates the heart's electrical power. Contracting when full, the right atrium pushes blood through a little door called the tricuspid valve – so named because of its three leaflets – into the right ventricle. Then, the right ventricle squeezes blood out of the heart and towards the lungs, and the tricuspid valve closes, preventing backflow into the atrium.

The systemic circulation is managed by the left heart. Oxygenated blood from the lungs pours into the left atrium until it's at capacity, sending its contents through the mitral valve, into the left ventricle. As the left ventricle starts to pump newly minted blood out and around the rest of the body, a healthy mitral valve will slam shut, preventing blood leaking back into the left atrium. But in someone with a floppy valve like mine, one or both leaflets overshoot, like the swinging doors in a saloon bar after a cowboy has made his showy entrance, allowing blood to regurgitate into the left atrium.

These facts feel indisputable. For a cardiac patient, conceiving of the heart as an electrically charged pump doesn't even require a leap of faith. Once a year, an envelope containing a Holter monitor lands on my doormat, and I stand in front of the mirror fastening electrodes to my chest, clipping the recording device to my waistband, happy to think of thousands of my heartbeats being traced while I go about my business. Every six months, I lie down in a shadowy hospital room, while an echocardiographer applies jelly and a probe to my chest, and maps the incremental progression of my disease, the usual quiet lub-dub amplified to a Niagara-like roar, my errant mitral valve flapping around on the grainy screen like a loose piece of washing on a line.

But anatomy is only obvious when you already know it. When English physician William Harvey first correctly explained how the heart works to a medical audience at the Royal College of Physicians in 1616, he was almost booed off the stage. It's natural to be suspicious of unfamiliar ideas when they threaten a status quo we've come to believe our best medicine depends on. But this is the beauty of anatomical history. It doesn't just bring a healthy wobble to our current dogma, but also reveals that what goes around, often comes around. Ostensibly radical theories may be found nestling among the debunked ideas of the past.

Early civilisations made no distinction between the mechanical and emotional aspects of the heart. Chinese parchments from 3,000 years ago described it as *xin zhu*, ruler of blood and spirit, while Hindu scripture from the eighth century BC presented the heart as both the physical hub and a person's emotional compass. The Egyptians' belief in the heart's symbolic value even extended to their death rites. When all other organs were removed from a corpse before mummification, this one was left in place to allow a special test. The dead body was believed to pass to the jackal-headed god Anubis, who placed the heart on scales, weighing it against the feather of truth. The heart represented the conscience and could speak against a person, while the rest of the body was there to appeal for mercy. Purity of heart granted passage to the afterlife while failure resulted in the heart being gobbled up by the monster Ammit, Eater of the Dead.

Things started to look more traditionally anatomical with the ancient Greeks, though there was nothing narrow about their approach either. Plato had faith in the heart as the seat of the soul, while Hippocrates mapped its four chambers. Aristotle, poring over a pulsating chick embryo, made the important discovery that the heart is the first organ to develop. But he was just as wedded to its poetic value, urging people to attend tragic theatre so as to purge their hearts through a cathartic encounter with terror and pity.

Amazing as it seems, between the ancients and Harvey's arrival, academic wisdom about the heart was dominated by the work of one man. Amalgamating scholarship from the Greeks, the Alexandrian physicians of the third and fourth centuries as well as Middle Eastern pioneers such as Ibn-al-Nafis, Galen's 9,000-page compendium of philosophy, medicine and physiology survived well beyond his own lifetime, a sort of meta-analysis of everything that had come before. Such was Galen's authority though, that no one thought to question his original contributions which, in the case of the heart, were retrograde. Disavowing Aristotle, Galen argued that the liver was the most important organ in the circulation and that blood was formed within it from the products of digestion, before overflowing into the right side of the heart. From there, he believed blood passed through imaginary holes in the septum to the left side, where it was warmed by mixing with air from the lungs and trickled out around the rest of the body.

Harvey was in his prime when he stood up at the Royal College, back from a fascinating spell in Italy, a couple of years away from being appointed personal physician to James I, just a few grey hairs on his big, clever head. But, looking down on the expectant faces of his erudite colleagues, he would have been aware he was up against fifteen centuries of Galenic dogma. So, how would he push through? By flaunting his academic prowess? By enlisting the support of other sceptics, such as Vesalius and Colombo? I don't think so. Harvey must have known his best chance was the very thing that made him different from the rest of this fusty community, hands-on experience and a beginner's mind. Amid the sneers and mutterings, I imagine him rolling up his sleeve.

The tourniquet experiment was one Harvey had practised on himself many times. Tying a handkerchief round his arm firmly enough that blood was prevented from returning to the heart through the veins, but not so tightly as to stop arterial blood flowing down his arm in the opposite direction, it was quite clear that the veins swelled up below the tourniquet but remained flat above it. By pressing blood out of a short length of swollen vein in his arm, he was able to demonstrate that the vessel only filled up again when blood was allowed to enter it from the end that was furthest away from the heart. His own teacher Fabricius had discovered the valves, without knowing what they were for. Harvey joined the dots, concluding their purpose was to ease venous blood flow smoothly towards the heart, as part of a continuous, one-way circulation.

By this point, Harvey's audience would have been captive enough for him to regale them with stories of his time in Padua, where the recent reintroduction of dissection had led to an explosion in new explorations of the human body. Harvey had enjoyed dissecting corpses as much as anyone, but what really interested him was how the heart behaved when it was alive, beating in real time. Finding the hearts of mammals too fast to observe, he had turned his vivisection to cold-blooded animals. By opening the tiny chests of toads, serpents, frogs, snails and lobsters, whose heartbeat was slower, Harvey had finally been able to describe something no one had previously noticed. Contrary to popular belief, the heart filled passively and contracted actively. Blood entered the atria, passed into the ventricles and was then squeezed around the body. The heartbeat was an act of propulsion.

In a learned sphere like medicine, it's easy to assume that false ideas will swiftly be replaced by true ones. So how did Galen's casuistry prevail for so many years?

Historical circumstances explain a certain amount. The Fall of Rome, in which many original texts were lost, meant Galen was working in a vacuum. The outlawing of dissection in 150 BC ensured his edicts went unchallenged, and the rise in Christianity elevated questions of the soul over matters of the physical body. But there's a less orthodox view that really tickles me.

In his fascinating essay on the heart, the late Jonathan Miller, who trained as a medical doctor before becoming a renowned theatre director, argues that the reason Galen's false anatomy of the heart took so long to be disproved was because of the lack of a satisfactory language for describing what was seen. Of course Galen likened the heart to a lamp, fed with fuel from the liver, and animating the blood, because that was in keeping with the technology of his day. It wasn't until the end of the sixteenth century, when mechanical pumps were invented for emptying mineshafts, extinguishing fires and supplying water to ornamental fountains, that the heart could even be imagined as a propulsive organ. The primary discrepancy between Harvey and Galen, says Miller, was never one of ingenuity or skill, but rather, of metaphorical equipment. It's what I've always thought. The truth of the body is as much about storytelling as it is about anatomy.

*

In 2019, Dutch researcher Hanno Tan published a paper in the *European Heart Journal* that sent shock waves far beyond the world of cardiology. After scrutinising 5,700 cardiac arrests in a single area of the Netherlands over a period of six years, he made the alarming observation that the outcomes between men and women were far from equal. Women whose hearts stopped in the community died more frequently than men in the same situation. Even those who reached hospital were less likely to receive both the necessary tests for diagnosing a heart attack and life-saving treatment. All in all, Tan concluded, the chance of a woman surviving to be discharged from hospital after a cardiac arrest in the community was half that of a man.

As Tan tried to tease out the reasons why women were dying at higher rates than men, he was initially confused, because the only explanation he could find – that women were less likely to receive life-saving defibrillation than men – was in itself baffling. On closer scrutiny though, things started to make sense. Of the women who had heart attacks at home, many simply didn't take their own symptoms seriously because they assumed heart attacks didn't happen to females. Even those who arrested in public, individuals whom you might have expected would attract immediate help from others, didn't receive it.

Heart disease is the most common cause of death in females globally. In the UK, a woman is twice as likely to die of a heart attack as breast cancer. But the story of heart disease is still one we associate with middle-aged men. The British Heart Foundation website is quite clear. Improving heart disease outcomes in women has to begin with a new narrative. But this isn't the only way we're starting to think very differently about the heart.

A few decades ago, a Japanese doctor called Hikaru Sato became fascinated by a specific group of patients arriving in the Emergency Room. On the face of it, these individuals appeared to be having heart attacks. Their symptoms were cardinal – chest pain, breathlessness and nausea. Their ECG tracings seemed characteristic too, and even their blood tests showed the raised cardiac markers that usually confirm an acute coronary event.

What piqued Sato's interest though was something cardiologists usually disregarded, his patients' stories. Something stood out: all of them described a recent and intense emotional experience. In a few, this was a major trauma like an assault, an earthquake or terrorist event. Mostly, it was something more humdrum, such as public speaking, a marital argument or nagging worries about finances. In a few cases, the symptoms followed happy occasions like a wedding, reunion or the start of a new job.

When Sato investigated these patients with the usual battery of heart tests, he found their angiograms were normal, with none of the furring of the arteries you would expect after a heart attack. The echocardiograms were weirder still, displaying a phenomenon he had never seen before. The left ventricles of this group were ballooning into a shape which reminded the Japanese doctor of a *takotsubo*, a traditional unglazed earthenware pot used by fisherman for catching octopus.

Takotsubo's cardiomyopathy, also known as Broken Heart Syndrome, is now well recognised among doctors, considered as a possible diagnosis in any patient presenting with acute chest pain, especially if they are female and postmenopausal. We know to watch out for it, and not to treat these patients with the heavy drugs and procedures that are only suitable for a heart attack. Asking patients about their emotions, something that never happened when I was learning medicine, is now commonplace. Harvey may have needed a new metaphor to articulate his revolutionary anatomy of the heart, but it has taken the ancient image of the *takotsubo* to wake us up to a disease that has probably been hiding in plain sight for generations. For all its magnificent achievements, modern cardiology has blinded us to what our ancestors knew. The heart doesn't just symbolically represent our feeling selves. The physical tissue of our heart, and our sentiments, are inextricably connected.

I am not the same person I was when I started writing this book and my body isn't the same body. I was still a young mother with a spring in my step, a doctor enthralled by a future treating other people's diseases. A decade later, I'm menopausal, haunted by memories of my child's illness, and with an ongoing heart condition. So, what has this time – in which I've added becoming a patient and the parent of a patient to my medical credentials – revealed about how we practise medicine?

We proceed on the basis that our facts are right, though it only takes a glance at medical history to realise they may soon be out of date. We rely on clinical protocols that claim to suit all bodies, when most of the data they're based on is taken from white male patients. Our Western healthcare systems persist in an outdated, post-industrial assumption that the body is a mechanical apparatus, when there is abundant medical evidence that our physical and emotional selves shouldn't be separated. If we're serious about improving our NHS, we have to take pause. We should teach medical students that any anatomy which doesn't take account of the person is false anatomy. We need to persuade managers who force doctors and nurses to work like machines, that human bodies aren't automata, that individual stories matter. We must provide doctors and patients with enough time to talk. For at no point are we more ourselves, or more adrift from ourselves, than when we are ill.

That said, it's taken becoming a patient to show me there are limits to how much we should expect even the best doctors to truly know us. I can say not a day goes by when I'm not grateful for the brain surgery that saved my son's life. I can tell you I've made peace with the long wait for heart surgery, with my cardiologist's view that – though my mitral valve inevitably will need to be repaired at some point – the right time for that is not now. But when it comes to more complex feelings about my child's body or my own, this language, with its clear, literal style and promise of complete-ness, just isn't enough. Not every experience can be conveyed directly. Some of our deepest and most diffi-cult moments can only be gestured at elliptically, or in fragments. They elude the cool codes of science.

But that's not the sum of it. There remains an essential contradiction in medicine, which all my attempts to merge the objective and subjective, the professional and personal, the intellectual and sensual have not shifted, which is that to understand disease, you have to stun it, freeze-frame the thing, make it still. To care for a patient, you have to step away from them. Knowledge and being can't be fully reconciled. Is this why my desire to fathom the human body remains as fierce as on that first day at medical school, why moments of revelation don't tend to come when, as a patient, I'm flooded with the primary experience of my own failing body nor when, as a surgeon, I step up to the operating table, tense with information, but somewhere in between, standing in a colleagues' theatre, or at some other momentous medical event, when all that's required of me is still observation, heartfelt attentiveness, a kind of quiet bearing witness?

Alive

It's the middle of the night, the city, the hospital, the theatre, the body. The heart surgeon takes the spreader, slots it into the chest cavity and winches it wide. Pushing the thymus across, he cuts open the pericardium and hitches it back with stitches. The entire body is exposed now but there is only one place to look. The whole world has shrunk to the focus of this thumping heart, the surrounding organs shivering with its transmitted beat.

Everyone waits. He lifts the heart up in both hands and gently squeezes it, checking with the anaesthetist that the donor's blood pressure is able to pick up quickly again after he's made it drop. Leisurely in this hiatus, he tapes the aorta, before looping thread around the superior vena cava, inferior vena cava and azygous vein. The other surgeons round the table prepare the kidneys, liver and lungs for explantation. In the side room, a nurse hammers bags of ice with a mallet and empties the slush into metal bowls.

When the phone rings – the recipient at the heart hospital on the other side of the country is on the table and they're opening her up – the atmosphere shifts, as if the very physics of the room are changing, solid to liquid. Bags of chilled University of Wisconsin Solution (UWS) are slung on stands at head and feet, and the scrub tables decked with bowls of ice. In the corner, the perfusionist sets up the Organ Care System. The cardiac surgeon inserts a cannula into the aorta and tethers it with a purse-string suture. The anaesthetist asks if everyone is ready, before setting the timer and announcing he is running in 30,000 units of heparin.

For three minutes, no one speaks or moves. Then the anaesthetist injects cardioplegia into the right atrium, and we all stand in silence as the heart struggles and finally stops beating. Almost immediately, everything becomes noisy and speeds up. The cardiac surgeon cross-clamps the aorta, stopping the blood supply that has been keeping the organs alive, announcing the beginning of what is known as the cold phase, which will continue from now until the point that a warm circulation can be restored. Every organ intended for transplant has its own lifespan of just a few hours, the heart the shortest of the lot. It's as if the starting gun has been fired for a race on which five lives depend.

To get things cold quickly, the surgeon must vent the body. He makes long slashes in the biggest veins so that all the warm blood that has been circulating can be emptied as fast as possible. Nurses squeeze bags of UWS through with freezing hands, and dump fish-market quantities of ice into the cavern of chest and abdomen. Blood brims in bottle after bottle, which I try to imagine, on their metal stack, as petals on a flower. Soon, all the red runs watery and the organs start to appear rinsed through and less lively, with the brown-grey cast of the dissecting room or anatomy book.

Carefully, the cardiac surgeon lifts the heart from the chest and bears it across the room to the Organ Care System, which looks bizarrely rudimentary, like a small bedside table with a transparent lid. I follow and stand beside him, watching as he fits tubes into the stumps of the main vessels and presses a switch to set the harvested blood running through the heart in a loop. Mini-defibrillator paddles are attached and, once he has shocked the heart a couple of times, it trembles and starts to beat again. I can hear the rhythmic thwack of it. On the other side of the room, the organs are coming out one by one and being packed on ice. But all I can do is stare at this heart, beating in its strange new home.

And, even now, I just can't fathom it. That this time yesterday, the dead body on the table was a whole man with a whole life, and absolutely no idea that in one blind moment, and with one wrong move, he would pass through a catastrophic set of stages: from brother to pedestrian-versus-lorry, from friend to patient, from son to donor. One day soon it will be me lying on the operating table, on bypass, chest cracked open, heart stopped, with a surgeon trying to repair my valve and save my life. Though when I think about it now, I don't feel fear, so much as a strange kind of longing.

At the window, the night sky shows the first glow of morning. The Organ Care System is wheeled from the room. The picnic boxes marked Organ-in-Transit follow one by one. Soon, five cars will carry these organs out across the country to five hospitals, where five patients and their families are waiting to start a new day. I step into the middle of the room, which was recently so busy. The donor is empty now, his skin baggy, yellow gut slack, the fork of the psoas muscle laid bare in the base of his abdomen. I move to the head of the table and look at the young man's face, where his childhood teddy still rests against his cheek. Next door, I hear the Specialist Nurse for Organ Donation quietly asking for shroud and body bag, soap and water. It's time for me to go home. But I'm not ready. So I pull up a stool and allow myself to sit, for just long enough to become aware of something I've never heard in the operating theatre before, the sound of my own heart.

Acknowledgements

Huge thanks are due to Claire Conrad for being the most amazing agent in the world and to Lara Agnew, my dream reader. To Bea Hemming, Jenny Dean and David Milner for their superb editorial advice and unwavering support. To Lynn Nesbit, Dan Franklin, Celia Johnson, Valerie Styker and Sam Guglani. To the teams at Cape, Godine and Janklow & Nesbit, especially Rhiannon Roy, Alison Davies, Rosanna Boscawen, Louise Navarro-Cann, Jamie Taylor, Rosie Palmer, Scarlet Chappell, Caroline Brink, Gretchen Crary and Olivia Everitt. To Colin Stolkin for taking a punt on me. To all the doctors, nurses, patients and other experts who have helped me so generously, in particular Kristian Aquilina, Paul Modi, John Skinner, Rob Pollock, Bill Edwards, Alice Roberts, Tina Rashid, Roland Morley, Colleen Kelly, Roshni Patel, Mats Branström, Sam Kemp, Edmund Jeffrey, Jennifer Rusby, Lisa Blundell, Melanie Morton, Andrew Perry, Justine Hextall, Nigel Heaton and Havi Carel. To Caroline Fahmy, Luiza Dinulescu and Flora Haxhia, for admin, childcare and

ACKNOWLEDGEMENTS

domestic relief. To Nikki Perry and Jemima Dhillon for yoga. To Emily Harper, Alice Mowlam, Lara Agnew, Lisa Rosen and Ben Weston for keeping me afloat. And to Ander and the kids, for their love.

About the author

Gabriel Weston is a surgeon, broadcaster and prizewinning author. Her *Sunday Times* bestselling debut, *Direct Red*, was longlisted for the Guardian First Book Award and won the PEN-Ackerley Award for Autobiography, while her novel *Dirty Work* won the McKitterick Prize. The presenter of several BBC TV series, including *Trust Me, I'm a Doctor* and *Incredible Medicine: Dr Weston's Casebook*, she currently works as a part-time surgeon and lives in London with her husband and children.